The Age of New Sweden

New A[...]
July 1999
Stockholm, Sverige

The Age of New Sweden

Livrustkammaren

Stockholm 1988

Published by the Royal Armoury with the aid of contributions from the Marcus
and Amalia Wallenberg Foundation and the Royal Armoury Foundation.

The front cover shows the "American medallion" from Skokoloster
Castle; the back cover shows the "European medallion".

Editors: Arne Losman, Agneta Lundström, Margareta Revera.
Translation: Bernard Vowles
Cover, production, layout: Inger Kåberg
Printing: Strokirks
Copyright © The Royal Armoury
ISBN 91-8759400-5

Foreword

Sven A Nilsson
   Imperial Sweden
   Nation-Building, War and Social Change   7

Allan Ellenius
   Visual Culture in Seventeenth-Century Sweden
   Images of Power and Knowledge   41

Gunnar Eriksson
   Science and Learning in the Baroque Era   69

Arne Losman
   Skokloster – Europe and the World in a Swedish Castle   85

Margareta Revera
   The Making of a Civilized Nation
   Nation-Building, Aristocratic Culture and Social Change   103

Caparison from gift of twelve horses and equipment presented to Karl XI by Louis XIV of France in 1673. The Royal Armoury. Photo: Göran Schmidt

Foreword

During 1988 the 350th anniversary of the founding of the colony New Sweden in North America will be celebrated in both Sweden and the U.S.A.

The colony, which lay on the Delaware River in what is now New Jersey, survived for only seventeen years, but many of the colonists remained there and contact with Sweden continued.

To mark the New Sweden '88 jubilee, a series of activities reflecting Swedish culture past and present is taking place in 1988 in all parts of the U.S.A.

Within the framework of these events a comprehensive historical exhibition of material from the age of New Sweden is being shown at two major American museums: the National Gallery of Art in Washington and the Minneapolis Institute of Art.

The exhibition "Sweden – a Royal Treasury 1550–1700" will include approx. 100 precious objects, regalia, arms and armour, textiles and costumes, together with various works of art connected with the Swedish royal family during the sixteenth and seventeenth centuries. The items belong to the Royal Armoury, the Royal Collections and the Treasury.

As the exhibition, with its regal theme, illuminates only a very narrow sector of seventeenth-century society – the monarchy – it has seemed desirable to present to an American public a number of other facets of the changing society of this extremely exciting period in Swedish history.

The Royal Armoury has therefore taken the initiative of commissioning this book and has asked a number of eminent Swedish scholars to give their view both of Sweden's political and economic history (Professor Sven A. Nilsson and Associate Professor Margareta Revera) and of certain aspects of its cultural history, namely the history of art (Professor Allan Ellenius) and of science and ideas (Professor Gunnar Eriksson). The Royal Armoury is administered by the same authority as Skokloster Castle, a quite unique seventeenth-century museum. This volume contains a special portrait of Skokloster by its Director, associate professor Arne Losman.

I wish to take this opportunity of conveying my sincerest thanks to these authors for their valuable contributions to this book.

In addition I owe a large debt for the admirable work put in by the specialist editors, associate professors Margareta Revera and Arne Losman. I would also thank Mrs Inger Kåberg of the Museum of National Antiquities, Stockholm, for her help and co-operation; she has been responsible for the design and layout of the book.

Finally I am grateful to our translator, Bernard Vowles, without whose help this book would not have been published.

The publication of this book has been made possible by the generous financial support of the Marcus and Amalia Wallenberg Foundation. I conclude by expressing my deep gratitude to this foundation, and its chairman, Count Peder Bonde, which has also contributed generously to other aspects of the work of the Royal Armoury, including the rebuilding of Queen Christina's coronation carriage.

Stockholm, 4 January 1988

Agneta Lundström
Director
The Royal Armoury/Skokloster Castle/
Hallwyl Museum

Imperial Sweden
Nation-Building, War and Social Change

SVEN A. NILSSON

The period usually known as Sweden's Age of Greatness was a relatively short one of a hundred years or so, depending on the landmarks chosen. In his books on the epoch, Michael Roberts has given it different boundaries – in one case 1621–1721, in discussing "Sweden's career as an imperial power", in another 1560–1718, for what he terms "the Swedish imperial experience". The state we are concerned with here is among the early modern states that emerge during the sixteenth and seventeenth centuries. Of these, one variety is what may be described as the military state, in which the demands of war and the armed forces are allowed to determine the construction of the state and the allocation of its resources. Here, it seems, Sweden is one of the most interesting examples, and the one that serves particularly well to illustrate the building up of the power of the state and the social changes that follow in the wake of this process.

In this essay I shall begin by outlining the main events of the period and go on to deal with developments during the two phases into which it naturally falls, with a division around 1680. May I first recall the course of events that forms the setting.

The Period in Outline

The expansionist foreign policy that is a mark of the Swedish Age of Greatness began as early as the mid-sixteenth century. Then and for a long time afterwards it looked east, having as its goal the control of the trade routes to Russia. The disintegrating Livonia of the Teutonic Order left a vacuum that its neighbours wasted no

time in exploiting. This applies to Sweden, to Poland and Denmark, and also to Russia, which did not intend to content itself with the role of passive producer country.

On the Swedish side, the policy of aggrandizement was initiated by Erik XIV (1560–68), and continued by his brothers, Johan III (1568–92) and Karl IX (1598–1611). Erik took Reval and Estonia in 1561 and then found himself at war with Denmark and with Poland, which claimed all the lands of the Teutonic Order for itself. Johan made peace with Denmark and was able to achieve a tenuous co-operation with Poland against Russia, which was always eager to strike out westward. For Sweden's part the war with Russia lasted until 1595, when Sweden succeeded in consolidating its possessions south of the Gulf of Finland and extended its border with Russia up to the Arctic.

That Sweden and Poland could co-operate was not due solely to their having a common enemy. There was also a dynastic connection as a result of Johan's marriage to the Polish princess Katarina Jagellonica, a connection with many consequences. One of these was the cultural effect of the court's links with the Polish and Italian Renaissance; Katarina's mother, Bona, was a Sforza from Milan. But what was most important was the claim she could lay both to the Italian inheritance from Bona Sforza and to Poland, where her brother Sigismund August was the last of the house of Jagello. These claims were a constant factor in Johan's foreign policy, and in 1587 he finally succeeded in having his son Sigismund, who had been brought up as a Catholic, elected king of Poland. In return he had to promise to cede Estonia to

The Swedish Empire. Provinces conquered after 1560 are shown by name and year of acquisition. Only the more enduring acquisitions have been marked.

Poland, a promise which was never kept but which reveals the conflicting interests that persisted below the surface.

After Johan's death, Sigismund ascended the throne of Sweden also. But his Catholicism and his impossible dual role as king of both countries caused difficulties that his uncle, Karl, made the most of to manoeuvre him aside and finally to depose him. This led to a long war with Poland and new Swedish activity in the Baltic territories. At the same time Karl made a drive for the Arctic Ocean, which had started to attract interest now that England and Holland had begun to use it as a route to Russia. Karl sought also to exploit internal dissensions in Russia and establish a client regime there.

Karl's restless aggressive foreign policy led to war with all those he had challenged: Poland, Russia and Denmark. It was left to his son, Gustav II Adolf (1611–1632), to bring these wars to a conclusion, making large territorial gains to the east. Peace with Russia in 1617 and an armistice with Poland in 1629 gave Sweden control of the entire Baltic coast down to the borders of the German Empire and the opportunity to levy tolls on all the trade of the region.

The armistice with Poland was negotiated with French mediation in order to facilitate a Swedish intervention in the Thirty Years' War, which had already been raging for a long time and in which the Emperor and the Catholic league were gaining the upper hand. An earlier attempt to intervene by Kristian IV of Denmark had been a fiasco. When Gustav Adolf landed in Germany in 1630 with a Swedish army the situation was favourable in that the Emperor had been persuaded to dismiss his commander-in-chief, Wallenstein, with military disorganization as a result. But the troops of the league were still in position and the Protestant states of Germany wavered. Moreover, there was a paralysing shortage of funds. In 1631, however, the problems were eased by French subsidies, and victory on the battlefield at Breitenfeld opened the way for the subsequent triumphant march towards the Rhine and southern Germany. At this juncture, Wallenstein was recalled, and in 1632 the two commanders confronted each other at Lützen. Sweden won the battle, but Gustav Adolf fell.

He was succeeded by his six-year-old daughter, Christina (1632–1654), during whose minority a regency of nobles ruled, with the chancellor, Axel Oxenstierna, at its head. Contrary to all expectations it managed to pursue the war and even to launch a surprise attack on Denmark from Germany. Peace treaties with Denmark in 1645 and Germany in 1648 gave rich gains in the form of provinces from Denmark–Norway and also a large part of Pomerania, together with the bishoprics of Bremen and Verden and the city of Wismar. The armistice with Poland had been renewed in 1635, although with the loss of customs revenue in Kurland and Prussia.

Sweden was now one of the great powers of Europe and, together with France, the guarantor of peace in Germany. But Christina's own foreign policy was somewhat erratic, and at times she sought to keep her options open with the Hapsburg camp. Her reason for doing this was her long-prepared conversion to Catholicism, which finally led to her abdication in 1654. Before this she had taken a succession of steps to ensure the transfer of the throne to her cousin, Count Palatine Karl Gustav, brought up in Sweden and the grandson of Karl IX.

Karl X Gustav's short reign (1654–1660) coincided with a crisis in eastern Europe that was precipitated by the weakness of Poland. He himself joined in by invading Poland in 1655, but after considerable early successes met opposition from Russia and Brandenburg–Prussia. By this time he had already turned his attention to Denmark, which had tried to capitalize on the opportunity for *revanche* but was instead compelled to accept the severe peace treaty of 1658, by which it lost Skåne and other border provinces. The very same year, Denmark was attacked again, but this time Holland came to her aid and the war became a lengthier one. While preparing for a fresh campaign, Karl Gustav died suddenly in 1660.

The heir to the throne, Karl XI (1660–97), was only

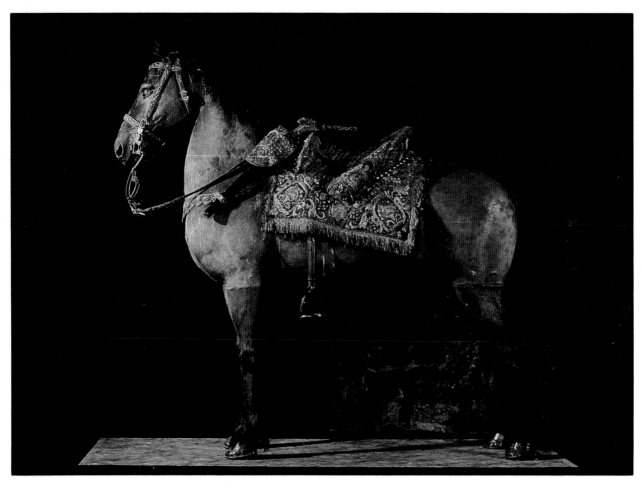

The horse ridden by Gustav II Adolf at the Battle of Lützen, 1632.
The Royal Armoury.
Photo: Göran Schmidt

The body of Gustav II Adolf is taken on board at Wolgast Harbour,
1633. Painting by Carl Gustaf Hellqvist. National Museum of
Fine Arts. On loan to Södermanland Museum.
Photo: Södermanland Museum

*Karl X Gustav. Portrait by
Sébastien Bourdon, c. 1653.
National Museum of
Fine Arts.
Photo: The National Swedish
Art Museums.*

four years old, and once again a regency of nobles had to tackle the situation. With French help Sweden succeeded in obtaining peace treaties that retained the majority of the territory wrested from Denmark and otherwise restored the status quo. The government concentrated thereafter on hanging on to its gains and maintaining peace in Europe, but was nevertheless drawn into an alliance with the aggressive France of Louis XIV. On his behalf Sweden had in 1674 to join in another major conflict in Europe, involving war with the north German states and with Denmark and Holland. Sweden was forced to withdraw from Germany, but Karl XI, who had now come of age, managed to retake Skåne, which had been invaded by Denmark. The treaties of 1678–79 restored to Sweden, with Louis' assistance, almost all the territory lost in Germany and in Sweden itself. Moreover Denmark had to reinstate Sweden's ally the Duke of Holstein in all his possessions.

These treaties were followed by far-reaching changes in Sweden, to which I shall return: absolutism, reduction (i.e. the repossession of landed estates by the Crown), commissions of inquiry and a radical military reorganization. Foreign policy, on the other hand, was restrained, based on the preservation of peace and balance in Europe and, now, on understandings with France's opponents. It was with their support that the security of Sweden and her Holsteinian satellite would in future be ensured.

When Karl XI died, his son Karl XII (1697–1718) was only fifteen, but he was soon declared of age. Within three years he was facing a concerted attack by Denmark, Russia and Poland. In Russia Peter the Great had embarked on a programme of modernization and in Poland Augustus II of Saxony was king, trying with his own army to assert his authority. With the aid of allies in the west, Denmark was brought to the negotiating table, the Russian army was annihilated at the Battle of Narva in 1700, and Augustus had to make a hasty retreat. But the war went on, soon involving the whole of northern and eastern Europe, while at the same time the other side of the continent was embroiled in the War of the Spanish Succession.

Poland was eventually obliged to remove Augustus from the throne and to replace him with Stanislas Lesczyński, a move that Augustus had to accept after Sweden marched into Saxony. This was followed by the great effort to subjugate Russia in 1708–1709, an invasion similar to the later ones by Napoleon in 1812 and Hitler in 1941, and as unsuccessful as theirs – failure in Karl's case, too, being partly due to an unusually severe winter. After the defeat at Poltava in 1709 he escaped to Turkey, where he stayed for no less than five years, during which time he twice managed to persuade Turkey to declare war against Russia. On his return after the famous ride to Stralsund in 1714, he once more faced all his original adversaries, of whom Augustus was reinstalled in Poland and Denmark was still looking for her chance. To these were soon added Brandenburg–Prussia and Hanover (now allied with England), both of them eager for Sweden's German provinces.

First from Pomerania, then from Sweden, Karl had now to wage a defensive war, during which first the overseas provinces were lost, then Finland. But he managed to raise new armies and marched on Norway with a large and well-equipped force in 1718. Here he was killed during the siege of the fortress of Fredrikshald on 30 November 1718. This time those who followed could not retrieve the situation, being compelled by the treaties of 1720 and 1721 to surrender nearly all the Baltic and German provinces and a part of Finland.

With this, Sweden's Age of Greatness was at an end. The enigmatic and headstrong Karl XII had given its long epilogue the character of a heroic drama, always captivating as such to both contemporaries and posterity. But Karl was not only an epic hero and Sweden's Age of Greatness was not only a history of wars and kings.

The Goals

For states of the kind typified by seventeenth-century Sweden, aggrandizement was virtually an end in itself,

and war was one of the principal means of realizing it. Sweden often tried to turn to account opportunities offered by the straits of its neighbours; the eastward thrusts bear frequent witness to this eye for the main chance. But these manoeuvres are also a part of a longer-term effort to dominate and enjoy the rewards of the rich Baltic trade. The extension of dominion along the coasts of the Baltic is evidence of this effort, as are the repeated attempts to gain control of trade on the Russian market. Both trading profits and tolls were at stake here, and with them the resources for the policies being conducted, resouces which, literally, had to be captured.

In the discussions that took place at the time, much was made of the need to ensure the kingdom's security, and in historical literature the security objectives have often been given a prominence equal to the trading ones. It is true that security considerations played their part, although taken in isolation they are a rather inadequate explanation for a policy of conquest. They acquire more substance if the concept of security is extended to mean the concern of the established great power to preserve what has been won. It then becomes convenient to proclaim a general goal of peace and balance between states or, in the language of seventeenth-century diplomacy, *securitas pacis*.

The Resources

The expansionist Swedish policy is remarkable in several ways, and not least in relation to the country's resources. The population was small. There cannot have been many more than a million people within the old borders of Sweden and Finland in the sixteenth century and about 2½ million in the imperial Sweden of the seventeenth century, with the conquered provinces included. In both cases, these are strikingly low figures in relation to the enormous activity generated and the comparatively large armies engaged and expended in the wars.

Nor were the financial resouces initially of any great

depth. Sweden was a land of small towns and poorly developed trade and industry. The mining of iron and copper was significant, admittedly, and of value to the Crown in various ways. But the agrarian sector was by far the most important, expanding in the late sixteenth century and the early seventeenth with the encouragement of rising prices. It was here that the Crown obtained its land revenues and the greater part of its tax income, including the extraordinary taxes that had first been imposed towards the end of the sixteenth century. These were later increased, and revenue was further augmented by levying them on individuals and households rather than on farms as previously. This taxation required some form of authorization at the *riksdag* or in local negotiations. The taxation system was to prove very adaptable and capable of expansion, and far superior to the rudimentary systems still in force in most of the countries of Europe.

However, the sectors of the economy to which most attention was devoted were those offering the most immediate prospects of profit. One such activity was mining, which expanded rapidly, with copper particularly favoured by the peculiar economic climate created by the Thirty Years' War. Ironworking was also a growth industry, with bar iron and also cannon and other munitions as its chief products. But the greatest hopes were pinned on trade, from which rich returns were expected and where the model was Holland, a small country but wealthy thanks to her flourishing commerce and financially powerful cities. Something similar could be made of Sweden, which would then have the economic strength to pursue the policies she wanted.

This is the context in which we must see the trade policy objectives of the expansion: the profits from Baltic trade should as far as possible be Sweden's. This did not happen: international commerce refused to take orders and Sweden had not the necessary capital or the trading position to enforce them. But the conquests brought new provinces with old centres of commerce and prosperous merchants and, more especially, the many tolls that could be collected. These resources had a significance greater than the sums they actually brought in. Their true importance lay in their function in the extensive credit operations on which the financing of the wars depended, operations in which the merchants of the cities were also induced to participate.

Indeed, this applies to Crown income generally: the crucial question was how it could be used to finance the wars.

Power structure and apparatus of government

The most powerful force in the Swedish state, as in most states in Europe at that time, was the king, and the trend, in Sweden as elsewhere, was towards an authoritarian system; however, formal absolutism did not arrive until the 1680s. Before this time, royal power was restricted by law and accession charter; at their side the monarchs had a council of the realm and the *riksdag*, in which nobility, clergy, burghers and also peasants were represented. Until 1622, moreover, there were royal princes with large duchies held in fief, who were also entitled to take part in the administration of the country.

For a long time this royal power was a highly personal one, exercised by the monarchs themselves when – it should be noted – they were not in the field. It was a part of the distinctive character of these monarchs – a primitive feature, perhaps – that they themselves took command in war, some of them very successfully.

Another characteristic Swedish feature was the presence, sharing or sometimes contesting power with the monarchy, of another political force, the aristocracy. It was the aristocracy that appointed the council of the realm and from whose ranks the regencies were drawn. This was not a rebellious feudal nobility of French or eastern European type but an aristocracy subscribing to a great extent to the same goal as the kings, that of building up a state strong enough for the requirements of war and great-power politics. It was also prepared itself to intervene and take over the apparatus of government.

During the sixteenth century this apparatus had consisted of a number of centralized administrative bodies and a local administration run by a large number of bailiffs. Its duties were mainly fiscal, the collection and supervision of the realm's revenue and expenditure. During the reign of Gustav Adolf this organization was expanded, as was the control system that is so characteristic of the Swedish military state of the seventeenth century. The central government departments grew in number and now assumed the collegial form that they were long to retain. To them was appended a regional administration led by the county governors, who were entrusted with the supervision of all local administration in their counties. The training of bureaucrats was also reformed, with the intention of modernizing and bringing greater discipline to the apparatus of government. The reforms extended to the armed forces, which acquired a more permanent form and their own administrative structure.

The clergy, too, were given important new secular duties during this period. Their task was to explain and gain acceptance for the wars and the burdens they brought to the population, and also to assist when taxation and conscription were reorganized on a household and individual basis. They had to draw up all the new lists that were needed and as an extra check to make out parish population registers. This is the start of the well-known Swedish population statistics, which begin here for the specific purpose of maximizing military recruitment and taxation.

Parallel with this building of the structure of the state, there is a concentration of authority in the hands of the king, although still within the framework of a separation of powers. In his accession charter of 1611, Gustav Adolf had undertaken to co-operate with council and riksdag, but in practice he had been able to bend them to his will. He had managed to form a close working relationship with the foremost member of the aristocracy, Chancellor Axel Oxenstierna. It was these two who built up the administration; the instructions were often Axel Oxenstierna's. His model was an administration with a carefully planned division of duties and with nobles in the leading positions, an administration that was expected to function autonomously. But it did not work out like that: Gustav Adolf never relinquished the means to intervene at crucial moments and he was often able to steer events in the direction he chose. Throughout the period of his rule, it was the king personally who held the reins of power. In other words, the military, the administration and the clergy were all at his disposal and became increasingly important during this period of national expansion.

Only after the death of Gustav Adolf in 1632 did Axel Oxenstierna have the chance to cement the administrative structure on which he had worked for so long. This he did in the instrument of government for which he obtained the approval of the riksdag in 1634. It left no room for the personal rule of the king; it was now the administration itself that took over, a permanently organized central and regional administration, in which the different bodies had clearly defined duties. At the head were the five high officers of state, regents during Christina's minority and each the head of an administrative board or kollegium. These now include the departments of state responsible for the armed forces – the war office and the admiralty. According to Axel Oxenstierna, these five administrative boards had been set up by the king "to rule the realm whether present or absent, alive or dead, so that the realm might be well superintended under a wise king and a foolish king would not at once bring it down". As we have seen, the instrument of government is not only concerned with the current regency but also draws up guidelines for a future system of aristocratic-bureaucratic government, with the king somehow curiously outside the scheme of things.

The system established by the instrument of government of 1634 set its stamp on the years that followed in many ways. During the relatively short periods of rule by a monarch who had reached the age of majority, the monarchs concerned certainly tried to introduce direct rule, but were often hampered by the permanent administrative routines. Indicatively enough, no monarch was willing to recognize the validity of the instrument

Axel Oxenstierna. Portrait by David Beck. Skokloster Castle. Photo: Bengt Kylsberg

of government. During the years of the regencies, on the other hand, it formed the basis of both government and administration. It was also a means of holdings the opposition in check.

This opposition was a new political force in Sweden. There had, it is true, been quite sharp reactions to the severe burdens imposed in the reign of Gustav Adolf, reactions which in the case of the peasants could take the form of veritable uprisings, usually at times of conscription. But on the political plane it is not until after the king's death that we find more organized opposition, usually among the three lower Estates of the *riksdag*. Here there was a general distrust of the aristocratic regency, which also tended to be blamed for the war levies. However, Axel Oxenstierna succeeded in partially curbing the opposition with the aid of the powers placed in his hands by the instrument of government. Bishops and county governors were instructed to supervise the elections to the *riksdag*, where the county governors also had the task of urging restraint on the peasants. Parish clergy, however, were unreliable: they could no longer be counted on to support the regime and often made common cause with the peasantry, as they also did with the burghers in the towns.

The opposition grew in strength during the reigns of Christina and Karl Gustav, when it sometimes co-operated with the monarch, and it remained an important power factor. As early as 1650 it presented its own finance programme, directed against the nobility, to which I shall later return.

The First Phase.
The Growing Military State and its Society

The most important organizer of the Swedish forces was Gustav II Adolf. He was the originator of a "soldiery ordinance", an incomplete document in which he expressed his ideas on how an effective war constitution should be formulated, and what it meant to a country. With a series of examples going back to the time of King David and of the Assyrians, Persians, Greeks and Romans, he tried to show that kingdoms flourish when they maintain their war constitutions. This had also been true of Sweden in times gone by, when the *göter* – actually the inhabitants of southern Sweden but to him the same as the Goths (*goter*) – struck terror into the world. In those days the whole population was armed, but now, he stated, war was waged by different means and a certain number of troops had therefore to be designated.

Gustav Adolf was arguing his case, of course, but in its historical retrospect it says quite a lot about the thinking underlying the military state as a system. What is at issue is the changeover, taking place at that time, between two methods of providing a supply of troops. Disregarding the cavalry, who could be attracted by various privileges, there may be said in earlier days to have been two methods of recruiting, the enlistment of mercenaries and the call-up for a shorter period of what was known in most countries as a "militia", i.e. an arms-bearing citizenry. The enlistment of mercenaries was costly, as was keeping them in service for any length of time. The militia was inexpensive, but could be used only for a limited range of duties and for the defence of its home area.

In the seventeenth century many countries therefore began to organize standing armies of native soldiers, compulsorily recruited by some form of conscription among the population. Lacking the resources for more widespread recruitment, Sweden had chosen this course quite early. By the middle of the sixteenth century attempts were being made to convert the militia into permanent companies and by about 1600 the point had been reached where these could be maintained by conscription, often of every tenth man of the rural population. However, the view that these troops were for the defence of their local district persisted, and there were often disturbances if they were required to fight abroad. There was also trouble when the government set about raising a militia as well, as in Finland in 1606, where every fifth man was called up over and above a conscription of every tenth.

This native army had seen service in the campaigns in

the east, and in Sweden it had once or twice faced Danish mercenaries, who had been unable to make their professionalism count in impenetrable border country. These wars with Denmark also showed that Denmark could only afford to keep professional troops in the field for a limited period; the Danes had not yet been able to establish a native army similar to the Swedish one.

Under Gustav Adolf's rule the national army was placed on a permanent footing and augmented by regular, increasingly efficient conscription. For its maintenance, farms were allotted and taxation in kind was prescribed according to rules resembling those later applied under the military allotment system (*indelningsverket*). Gustav Adolf also experimented to find a satisfactory balance between pikes and firearms, which formed the basis of new tactics. These were tested in exercises in Sweden, about which, unfortunately, little is known, but which clearly produced results: there is no other way of explaining how newly recruited forces could be pitted against Continental troops. But it was to be several years before Gustav Adolf dared risk his new army in pitched battle.

Heavy losses were still sustained, however, as a result of the devastating epidemics that swept through the Swedish forces on foreign soil. This is why the sorely felt conscriptions had to be repeated so often, and also why Gustav Adolf turned increasingly to the use, in addition, of foreign mercenaries. In 1630, before the war in Germany, his fighting strength consisted of 41,000 Swedes and 31,000 foreign troops, and there were 3,000 men in the navy. The national forces now had to form a reserve at home and in the provinces and also to make up the expeditionary force to Germany. The men of the navy were also Swedish.

In Germany the Swedish units gradually suffered the usual depletions and had to be replaced with new men recruited locally. It was also German mercenaries who made up the new Swedish armies that were raised. Germany was the great recruiting market and the theatre of war was expected to bear its costs.

We find the same pattern in the later Continental wars. The expeditionary forces were mainly Swedish and they were reinforced with large units of locally recruited mercenaries. In the parallel wars fought with Denmark in the 1640s and 1650s, it was again the mercenaries who put in the main thrust from the south, while Swedes were used against Norway and Skåne. In the Danish wars the navy was also active.

The war of the 1670s also began with a Swedish expeditionary force, which sailed over to Germany in 1674 and was supplemented by recruitment there. As usual, the war was expected to be self-sustaining. But this time the army was forced to retreat and was largely lost. Denmark now took a hand and attacked from Norway and Skåne. For the first time for many years the main war front was at home in Sweden and it was on domestic resources that it had to be sustained. New Swedish forces had to be committed, and this was not done easily. The national army was in poor shape, the units were not up to full strength and they were inadequately trained. The navy, too, was ill-equipped and undermanned, and much of it was lost in the war. It was experiences of this kind that led to changes in the military system in the 1680s.

Under the system with which we have hitherto been concerned, it was expensive to start a war; large sums were needed for armament and recruitment. The navy also cost a great deal in new vessels and equipment. These large lump sums could never be provided within the framework of the Swedish budget; most of the money had to be borrowed against future income, usually from tolls and copper. This was supplemented by what could be scraped together from taxes and contributions from the overseas provinces. The lenders were initially mainly private individuals such as the Dutchman and industrialist Louis De Geer, who contributed to both the German war and the Danish war of 1643–45. In the 1650s and 1670s support came chiefly from another direction, the Crown revenue collectors, who in keeping with the general practice of the time granted large loans against security in funds that they themselves managed, usually tolls.

As was to be expected, the scene of the fighting was made to provide a great deal in the form of maintenance, contributions and confiscations of various kinds. But in practice these sources of income were never sufficient and had always to be supplemented from elsewhere, usually with war subsidies from allies and with Swedish customs and copper revenues. Swedish taxes were spent primarily on the border wars with Denmark and Russia. The same happened in the 1670s, when the areas of Sweden ravaged by the war had to be responsible for the support of the armies. The navies that were active in all the Swedish–Danish wars also cost large sums which were raised in Sweden.

Another aspect of the financing of the wars that has to be mentioned – indeed possibly the essential one – was the credits, all the advances and loans that were necessary in order for the system to function. Loans were raised on any income of reasonable regularity, subsidies, tolls, copper revenues, contributions etc., so that these items were often overmortgaged when they fell due. The result was outstanding claims that were steadily postponed and rescheduled. The granters of credit were many. Most of them were in central positions, in many cases those people who covered the costs of mobilization. Others were the financiers, some of them located in Holland, who dealt with copper exports. Swedish agents in other financial centres also played their part, being expected to obtain loans with their own resources and their own credit. An early example here is Johan Adler Salvius, in Hamburg, who played a major role during the Thirty Years' War and later became a councillor of the realm and a baron. Another important group consisted of the merchants who delivered to the armies. One of these was Melchior Degingk, who was the biggest supplier and creditor of the Swedes in the final stages of the Thirty Years' War and lent large amounts to the Swedish Crown. He had to wait for his money, but he became a Swedish nobleman under the name of von Schlangenfeldt, and eventually he, too, became a baron. We find the same combination of supplier and creditor in all the major Swedish cities, and many of them were similarly rewarded for their services with ennoblement.

There were also claims of a different kind, for unpaid wages. The troops were often put on short commons, which led to a backlog of claims and also, in the case of the officers, to demands for gratuities. The gratuity (recompens) was a part of the system and, to the officer, just as important as the salary. In a war using mercenaries, such a situation could not be allowed to continue for long without risk of mutiny. Such a crisis arose in the Swedish armies in the south of Germany in 1633. It was resolved by a German financier, Christoff von Brandenstein, who advanced millions in return for a promise of extensive lands seized by Sweden in southern Germany, which he never received. His dealings with the Swedish Crown were his ruin, just as his contemporary Hans de Witte was ruined by Wallenstein.

For an economy of this kind, the problems came with peace, when there was no longer a war theatre to be saddled with the costs. Loans had to be repaid and officers and troops had to be satisfied. If this were not done, there would be a total loss of credibility on the credit and recruiting market. This problem of demobilization is well known, but not all of its implications have been apparent.

Some of them are illustrated by the circumstances following the Treaty of Westphalia, under which Sweden received 5 million *riksdaler* with which to satisfy her troops. These therefore received large sums, as did creditors and officers of higher ranks. But the funds were still insufficient, and the balance of their claims had to be settled within the state of Sweden. In other words, it was expensive to conclude a war, even more expensive than to begin one. This has a bearing on the question of how costs were distributed between the scene of operations and extraneous contributions, particularly from the home country. It is usually assumed that the theatre of war bore the brunt, but this overlooks the large proportion of the costs that were only met afterwards at home. This also affects the calculations that have been made, in Sweden and elsewhere, of the volume of expenditure. These are often based on the records of payment from different sources for purposes connected with the war. Here, too, the error arises from the various claims that always existed, but were never settled promptly, seldom settled before the end of the war, and sometimes not settled at all.

This brings us on to the Swedish national economy. This was, as has already been shown, under severe strain from the various costs of the war; when in addition all the costs of demobilization were added, the situation could be considered serious. This was not in itself remarkable in the Europe of the period: most states had had their finances ruined by war. But Sweden was an extreme case in the magnitude of the discrepancy between the country's limited resources and the demands of the heavy military sector, including a substantial fleet, a large national army and, at times, a large number of mercenaries, maintained in a state of war readiness for long periods.

This is not the place for a detailed discussion of the problems of state finances, and I shall confine myself to those sectors which relate more directly to demobilization. The most important problem was the debts, which the contemporary rollover mechanism often postponed until peace was restored. Some were dealt with by simply disowning them, as were Brandenstein's claims. But a start had to be made on paying off most of them. In 1648, war indemnity enabled settlements to be made with Salvius and Degingk. But they did not get all that was due; the rest had to be raised in Sweden in the 1650s. Louis De Geer had the same experience, being paid only later and in Sweden. Those who lent money at the time of the big mobilization of 1655 got most of their money back in the late 1650s, by which time, however, there were numerous new creditors, who had to be paid in the years that followed. Payment was made from various Swedish sources of income, or in the form of landed estates, sold or pledged, often in the conquered provinces or, after 1660, in Skåne. After the treaties of 1679, however, there were no new foreign provinces to exploit, and certainly no war indemnities.

But there was also the problem of wages and gratuities, for which there were only the resources of the kingdom of Sweden itself to draw on. These were duly utilized in the form of donations of hereditary estates, by now one of the normal methods of rewarding the nobility in Sweden. Gustav Adolf had made such donations, particularly in the Baltic territories, where the higher nobility of Sweden received its reward for its contribution to the policy of expansion. After the Treaty of Westphalia, there followed a new wave of donations of land, this time very substantial ones. These have generally been seen as a concomitant of war, but there has also been frequent criticism of what has been regarded as prodigality, especially on the part of Queen Christina.

However, a closer analysis of the registers of donations and indemnity payments shows that there was in fact a system, a way of paying for war service and at the same time binding the nobility to the state. Among the recipients is a group that received extremely large amounts of land and sums of money, namely the councillors of the realm, officers of high rank and civil servants. Officers of lower rank received considerably less, whether in indemnity payments in Germany or in donations of land at home. One can also discern a definite effort to tie foreign officers and creditors to Sweden with Swedish landed estates and titles. It should also be mentioned that the newly acquired provinces were squeezed to the limit, just as the Baltic territories had been earlier.

The system clearly acknowledged the idea that service merited a recognition of this kind, a recognition which for high-ranking officers was more important than their salary. There was also a corresponding view of the obligations of the recipient of a donation. This is encountered in 1634, for example, in a discussion by the council of the realm of a mission to Russia. The appointee, Henrik Fleming, complained that the allowance for his expenses was too low, which aroused great annoyance in the council, as he had, it was pointed out, received a large benefice from the king and ought not therefore to shirk his bounden duty.

The donations, together with the purchases of estates by the nobility that took place at the same time (in some cases to be set off against claims), represented a tremendous increase in the nobility's holdings of land. Their extent may be expressed as the proportion of the land in the country – stated in *jordemantal*, the contemporary unit of land measure – that was in the hands of the nobility in 1654, when the transfers of landed estates reached their maximum. The figures apply mainly to Sweden and Finland within their old borders.

	Mantal of the nobility	Total
Sweden	39,632	60,750
Finland	14,323	24,539
Total	53,955	85,289

Not all the donations from the last year of Christina's reign have been included. The holdings of the nobility ought therefore to be rounded up to about two-thirds of the total, with the new acquisitions accounting for the lion's share. From this time on, the proportional distribution of the estates remained virtually unaltered: new donations were balanced by the limited reduction (reclamation by the Crown) that took place. It now conformed quite closely to the pattern common in feudal countries, with the nobility clearly the dominant landowning class.

This huge transfer of property was, as we have seen, both a precondition and a consequence of the military policy. It was a method of ensuring the service of the nobility, particularly its war service, that was peculiar to Sweden. But it created new problems that were to have a far-reaching effect in the future.

All the landed estates of the nobility were exempted under its privileges from regular taxation and also, after 1644, from the older tier of extraordinary taxes. To varying degrees these estates were also excused from conscription and similar levies. In other words, an increase in the number of noble estates implied a decline in the revenues and dues that went to the Crown. It tended also to give rise to social problems; a large part of the transfers involved the freehold farms of the peasantry. In these cases the transfer concerned not the proprietary right but only the taxes to which the Crown waived its claim. But there was a risk that the nobles would regard these farms, too, and their owners, as their own lands and peasants.

It is in this context that we have to consider the opposition of the three commoner Estates of the realm. This had already made itself felt during Christina's regency and in the 1640s it had taken the form of vigorous attacks on the nobility, culminating in the protests at the *riksdag* of 1650. Here it was argued that the Crown ought to take back its landed estates and live on their dues, rather than on the new taxes that were weighing so heavily on the commoners, particularly as the nobles were also appropriating the tax revenues from the newly exempted lands. The nobility was accused of grinding the faces of the peasants and driving off those who still owned their farms. The accusations have long re-echoed through the historiography and continue to do so.

Axel Oxenstierna and his fellow nobles had little time for such a message. They heaped sarcasm on the belief that the state could function as in the old days, when the king lived off his landed estates. Their programme was very different: the Crown should not concern itself with taxes on land but should base its finances on tolls and other indirect taxation, and on the proceeds of commerce in general. Leaving the landed estates to the nobility was if anything an advantage: they would then be better managed and the general weal would increase.

For a long time the policies pursued were largely those desired by the aristocracy. But the income to which most importance was attacked, from tolls, copper and other indirect taxes, was swallowed up by the wars and the payment of debts. At the same time, tax revenues dropped as a result of the alienation of estates. The consequence was a growing deficit in the domestic budget, a deficit that had to be made up by temporary measures. These included the cutting of salaries; eventually it became the exception for salaries to be paid in full.

The difficulties were such that new remedies had to be tried. One of these was the one proposed by the commoners: reduction. It was revived every time they were faced with new tax demands, and in 1655 Karl X Gustav carried out a limited reduction, applying to estates of certain categories. Until these lands were surrended, those who had received donations were to pay a corresponding revenue to the Crown, to make up the shortfall in the domestic budget. From then on, the decision of 1655 was taken as having established a principle, and the desirability of extending its application as far as possible was argued forcefully.

In consequence of this, it proved more or less impossible to impose new taxes on the three commoner Estates of the realm. Instead, it was the nobility and its peasants – of all categories – who had to pay. The peasants suffered in that many of their privileges were lost, even the extensive ones enjoyed by the farms nearest the manor houses. The same applied to their exemption from conscription, which could not be preserved either. For the nobles this restricted the chance of collecting land revenues themselves.

As if this were not enough, the nobles had also to renounce the personal tax exemption that was the very essence of their nobility. Time after time they had to agree to large contributions assessed in proportion to their land holdings. This was an alternative to reduction, but an alternative which, like the curtailment of privileges, inevitably divided the nobility. For it affected all tax-exempt estates, whereas a reduction applied only to the recent donations, and these were mainly in the hands of the titled families. The antagonism is clearly expressed in a submission by Maurits Posse to the *riksdag* of 1678: "It would be well," he said, "if we might for once find ways to escape our contribution and our privileges might remain untouched. There are many who possess and withhold the Crown's estates and incomes; as long as they are beyond His Majesty's reach we cannot hope to avoid our contribution, nor be sure of retaining our privileges."

The wars and the needs of the military also had other implications for the groups making up Swedish society. Some of them require mention here.

One of these consequences was the emergence of a group of businessmen, financiers and large-scale merchants who ran the ironworks and the war industry and also the copper trade and large-scale commerce generally. This is where we find those who provided supplies for and financed the wars and the traders who satisfied the demand of the time for status-symbolizing luxuries, sought by the royal family and the aristocracy as much as by well-to-do burghers. (I refer the reader to Margareta Revera's contribution to this volume.) Many of this group were of foreign origin and had far-flung business contacts. All had links of various kinds, including credit arrangements, with the world of international commerce and were thus able to bring in the necessary working capital. The members of this group are difficult to assign to their place in Swedish society with its Estate system. They may best be considered a wealthy burgher class with interests that distinguished big merchants from other burghers of the towns and ennobled financiers from the nobility in general.

The changes that have provoked most discussion are those involving the nobility and the peasants and appearing most obviously to be a result of the transfer of landed property. This discussion has long been coloured by the impression left by the many charges levelled against the nobility during the struggle between the Estates of the realm. It is true that, except in historical novels, the nobility of the seventeenth century is no longer depicted indiscriminately as a pack of unmitigated harassers of the peasantry. But the notion persists of a nobility threatening the freedom of the peasants, especially of those peasants who had come under the authority of the nobility while retaining the ownership of their farms. Historical materialists sometimes portray this period as one of "refeudalization", in which the peasants had now to hand over their entire surplus to their feudal lords.

The real hardship of the peasantry, however, came from the conscriptions that hit them year after year, taking the rural workforce abroad and destroying much of it there. But here the interests of the nobles and the peasants lay in the same direction, and the system that took such a heavy toll of the country's manpower was abandoned as soon as the resources were available for using mercenaries, who were clearly more durable.

Concerning the time that followed, which has been called the period of aristocracy or – at times – the feudal era, new studies show a state of affairs almost diametrically opposed to that traditionally imagined. The peasants of the nobility did not suffer oppressive conditions compared with those of the Crown peasants, and the position of the peasant freeholders seems to have been respected even when they had come under the authority of the nobility. The restraint of the nobility obviously has its roots in the strong position of the commoners after the middle of the seventeenth century. That the tax burden was heaved onto them is a stereotype owing most to the hyperbole of propaganda generated in the quarrels between the Estates.

But in another respect there was a change in the position of the peasants of the nobility, the tenants. Since the sixteenth century the Crown had begun to increase the taxes of its peasants in times of war, and gradually they found themselves paying as much in extraordinary taxes as the peasant freeholders, whereas previously they had paid only half as much. The nobles then followed the Crown's example and took as much from their own peasants. The effect of this was that during the seventeenth century all these tenants saw their relative position deteriorate, despite the fact that they had smaller farms than the freeholders. The alienation of estates by the Crown had brought nearly all of them under the nobility, and they must have had difficulty in making ends meet. The favoured group appears instead to be the peasant freeholders, although they were depicted by contemporary propaganda and in later literature as so sorely tried.

The nobility itself may be classified in various ways: Swedish and foreign, old and new, higher and lower, military and bureaucratic. Comparing landlord and office-holding nobles has less point: in Sweden they almost all held some form of office. On the basis of their interests, I prefer to deal with them as two main groups. One consisted of those possessing large landed estates, the titled nobility, whose members could count on the leading civil and military positions. It was they who had received most of the donations. The other consisted of civil servants, officers and others who did not have very extensive lands and had not received large donations. The latter had nothing against a reduction, if it relieved them from further contributions and at the same time opened the way to donations in the future.

The situation becomes more complicated when salaries are considered. Cuts in their salaries were a severe setback to the bureaucrats of the lower nobility, especially at a time when land revenues were decreasing as a result of increasingly heavy taxation. But the higher ranks of the nobility were also affected. They had very high nominal salaries; if these were lost or cut, a situation could arise where they might not necessarily lose by a reduction, if the repossession of land enabled the Crown to pay their salaries in full.

There is also, however, the question of how the higher nobility managed its lands. It might have been expected that the massive increase in manorial estates would involve a changeover to owner-management in place of the earlier system of tenancy alone. But this did not happen. The main concern was, as Margareta Revera shows, status in the form of luxuries and the building of palatial residences, in which huge sums were invested. The way was shown by the head of Karl XI's regency, Magnus Gabriel De la Gardie, who was the biggest builder of the period. He overreached himself with his expenditure and he was not alone in this. For in

Sweden the epoch of the nobility and of manorial building came at the wrong time. It came when agricultural prices were stagnating or falling. It was then that all the mansions were built that now stand as a monument to the undermined finances of the nobility.

In these circumstances, it is not difficult to see parallels with the groupings in other countries that have featured in the debate on the crisis of the seventeenth century. In Sweden, too, there was a higher nobility, whose position was becoming precarious. Other groups were rising: the bureaucrats of common birth or from the lower nobility, and the groups from the ecclesiastical and burghers' Estates who were emerging as the leaders of the commoners. We also have a new class of wealthy merchants engaged in trade, mining and munitions and in business with the Crown. All could see their way blocked by the formerly dominant higher nobility.

So parallels did indeed exist. But there were also marked differences that complicate attempts to fit events in Sweden into any conventional interpretative model. One of these differences was the strong position of the Swedish peasantry, among whom the freeholders had, if anything, become stronger during the "feudal era". Another was the heavy military sector and the part played by the wars in the transfer of resources to the nobility. A third was the permanent apparatus of control, with the aid of which even regencies were able to maintain government power.

These were also the factors that determined the behaviour of the sovereign. The reigns of Christina and Karl Gustav had shown that the non-noble Estates quickly fell into line once the monarch took over from the regency, and the apparatus of government was normally at his or her disposal. The problem was the nobility. Its leading stratum had formerly run the state, along with the monarchs, or at times in conflict with them. As far as the rest of the nobility is concerned, all that can be stated here is that the antagonisms of the period before monarchic absolutism concerned lands and privileges more than power and influence.

The Second Phase.
Change of System and Consolidation

The *riksdagar* of 1680 and 1682 and the decisions that led to monarchic absolutism, reduction and commissions of inquiry form the subject of a copious literature dealing with both the changes and their effect on society. Here, too, the military requirements may be presumed to have played an important, maybe a crucial, role. Let us examine events from this viewpoint.

After the war which had recently come to an end, a new generation of creditors and officers was waiting to present its claims. But there was little with which to satisfy them; resources in lands and revenues had been exhausted in the settlements that followed earlier campaigns. Even less were there resources for the military reform that was now being planned. The navy had to be rebuilt and the army reorganized: the war had exposed the inadequacies of the previous system. In Europe, standing armies were being established, composed mainly of mercenary or conscripted troops and reinforcements drawn from various forms of militia. Raising and arming such forces was cheaper than the old system with its enormous recruiting costs. But once the troops were there, they had to be maintained, in peace as in war.

In Sweden the budgetary proposals for 1680, i.e. the estimates of future expenses and income, show that all the requisite military expenditure had been included and also that it would have been impossible to provide for it within the existing budget. In previous times of financial difficulty, the alternatives had been reduction and the levying of contributions. An argument in favour of a reduction was the existence of the military allotment system, which, although still far from perfect, maintained the national army and supplied the manpower for the fleet. If it were to be extended, a substantial restoration of landed property to the Crown was necessary. But it would also be possible to introduce more taxes and then take more from the nobility and their landed estates or – as in Brandenburg–Prussia – pass part of the military burden to them.

Tactics at the *riksdag* of 1680 were carefully prepared. The royal proposal spoke in general terms of the need for appropriations for the navy and the army and for the settlement of debts. Among the nobles, one of the king's men, Hans Wachtmeister, pushed through a proposal for an inquiry into the administration of the previous regency, which seemed likely to produce funds. When the commoners then suggested a new reduction and this aroused the protests of the nobility, he himself moved that all the largest donations should be repossessed. This would affect what was now quite an isolated group of the highest ranks of the nobility, and the motion was carried amid tumultuous attacks on those who were holding "the property of the realm", attacks during which the alternative of contributions was once again rejected. The background is – as has already been observed – the peculiarly Swedish distribution of landed estates, where a large part of the lands of the nobility was recently acquired and in the hands of the very highest ranks of the aristocracy.

Once this had been done came the next act, which brought a proposal for funds for the navy and for fortifications. This was entirely unexpected: the minutes of the nobility speak of "a short silence in the chamber" when this had been read out. But there was no way out. The nobles had to go along with yet another personal contribution, which would be followed by many more; they were never to regain their personal exemption from taxation. And this time the commoner Estates of the realm were also prevailed upon to agree to new taxes.

The Estates had thus opted for a reduction in the hope of escaping new taxation. But they got both.

Events continued in the same vein. The *riksdag* of 1682 was concerned with finding the wherewithal to pay off the debts. The commoners proposed an extended reduction, but the nobility was determined to save what was left. The king then asked precisely what rights were invested in him by law. He received the answer he wanted: he had the right to "take back grants and give grants". With this he had full authority to decide on the question of reduction, with or without the consent of the nobility.

The implementation of the decisions was entrusted to various commissions, who were ordered to carry out the reductions and to reorganize the military allotment system. Another commission was to determine the responsibility of the regency and whether it could be made liable for repayment. It was also to settle the claims of creditors and examine the sales and hypothecations of landed estates that had taken place. Yet another commission had been appointed to investigate whether the manors of the nobility and their neighbouring farms had received their privileges legitimately. To the nobility this was as sensitive an issue as a reduction: it concerned the most valuable part of their land holdings and one where abuses were many and the risk of repercussions was considerable.

At the *riksdag* of 1682 the peasants were also made to define their position with regard to the new organization of the army. They then undertook to procure and maintain manpower for the infantry regiments in accordance with certain standards and in return for exemption from conscription. If this were not done, conscription would be reintroduced on stricter lines. In either event, the peasants of the nobility would – in spite of their privileges – have to achieve as much as other peasants. The decision would be permanently binding, irrespective of future decisions of the *riksdag*.

Thus the Crown had now repossessed the very large complex of landed estates that had once been the reward of the nobility for its services and its war efforts. Moreover, the inquiry into the administration of the regency resulted in many nobles having to pay in land. The nobles had also been induced to grant a hefty new contribution, and the non-noble Estates of the realm had likewise had to accept new taxes over and above those believed in the middle of the seventeenth century to represent the absolute limit to the taxation burden. And in addition – in some respects most remarkably of all – the procurement of manpower and the cost of the troops had been removed from the control and voting of the *riksdag*.

With these decisions, the new regime had gained the means to carry out its costly programme of military reform. Behind the actions stood an autocratic monarch, whose priorities were in direct conflict with the interests of the higher nobility. But there were also other interests involved, ones which could benefit from the change.

The conventional view of the society of the era of reduction and military allotment was formulated fifty years ago by the distinguished economic historian Eli Heckscher. As he saw it, military allotment tied the Swedish economy to an antiquated system, ill-fitted for wartime, for a long time to come. The reduction was justified on the grounds of national finance and was carried out solely with financial considerations in mind. It removed the threat to the freedom of the peasants but otherwise paid little heed to the interests of the peasantry. The nobility lost almost half of its holdings of land but showed a remarkable ability to hang on to the more valuable portion, the manors with their attendant farms. Within the nobility, however, changes took place, in that new groupings of bureaucratic or mercantile origin obtained property and titles and exploited the opportunity to acquire lands cheaply.

This view has been reassessed in several respects as a result of more recent research. There have also been attempts at a more integrated approach, chiefly by historical materialists. These usually see reduction as a revolution within the framework of the system, in which an aristocracy was replaced by a bureaucracy of the untitled nobility, but without any other change in the feudal system in general. However, the reduction and the military allotment system are considered to have constituted the preconditions for a new society. Perry Anderson, in dealing with absolutism, not only emphasizes that the feudal structure was retained in Sweden but also points out that this was essential if the acquiescence of the nobility was to be obtained. Other historical materialists have stressed the revolutionary character of the change:

they see it as having left the field free for the bourgeoisie and thus entailing what from this viewpoint is designated the "bourgeois revolution".

I shall consider this later. Bur first a few figures. The demand for compensation arising from the inquiry into the regency alone amounted to 4 million Swedish *daler*. The reduction is often assessed in terms of the regular revenues restored to the Crown, 2 million *daler* a year, of which 700,000 *daler* was from Sweden and Finland within their old borders. The overseas provinces contributed most – Estonia and Livonia as much as Sweden and Finland. An account of the amount of land, expressed in *jordemantal*, may give a more graphic picture. The figures for 1654, quoted earlier, may be compared with the corresponding ones for the year 1700, although the latter relate to a redefined *mantal*, and the comparison must therefore be based on the percentages. The figures apply to Sweden only, within the same borders as before.

| | Property of the nobility | | Total | |
	Mantal	Percentage	Mantal	Percentage
1654	39,632	65.2	60,750	100
1700	15,976	31.4	50,899	100

In Sweden proper, therefore, the nobility had lost more than half of its onetime land holdings. This must have been equally true in the kingdom as a whole: the reduction in the overseas provinces was, as just stated, very extensive.

From the point of view of the national finances, the figures give an approximate measure of what the Crown once more had at his disposal. In the case of the nobility, however, they are slightly misleading; its true losses were less than one might expect from the figures. The precise situation becomes apparent from an examination of the way in which the reduction was carried out and the repossessed property was used.

In Sweden and Finland there was a close connection between, on the one hand, the demands of military organization and, on the other, the reduction and the commission of inquiry into whether the country houses of the nobility (and their farms) were legally entitled to their manorial privileges. The military allotment system needed a large number of farms for the maintenance of the cavalry and as dwellings for officers of all branches of service. It also required a solid local basis for the provision of soldiers, i.e. peasants in units of a few farms each who undertook to supply soldiers for the infantry and seamen for the navy. These needs determined what was reclaimed by the Crown and how, and where there were conflicts of interest, priority was given to the cavalry with its enormous need for farms. There was a parallel connection with the inquiry into the award of manorial privileges: the inquiry was intended to limit the number of manors with farms around them that were exempted from taking part in the provision of soldiers. For the same reason it was prescribed that no new manors could be established: the military organization must not be interfered with. It was in fact often the same officials who had locally to administer military allotment system, reduction and commission of inquiry.

Such was the situation in Sweden and Finland. In the foreign provinces repossession was even more drastic, but the landed estates nevertheless remained in the hands of the nobility, on lease. The explanation is clearly that in the provinces neither the military allotment system nor the local provision of soldiery was established and the estates were never needed for these purposes. Presumably there was also some attempt to take account of the Baltic and German nobility, which could not be entirely alienated. The leases were soon made permanent and the rents can thus be regarded as a standing charge for the estates.

Another precondition of the new society was the salary system, and first and foremost the fact that salaries could now be paid out. Not only those allotted to officers and soldiers, who often collected them themselves, but also the cash salaries that were more important to the higher officials and in the central government departments. They were, of course, subject to tax – after 1682 the contributions consisted of one-tenth of all salaries – but most of the money could usually be made available. This meant a great deal, not only to the lower civil servants but perhaps most of all to their higher and very highest ranks. It was their high wages that enabled them to bear all the strains of the reduction and the commissions of inquiry.

It is against this background that we have to consider the social consequences. As far as the peasants are concerned, their conditions can hardly have been improved by the reduction. Traditional opinion on this is that peasant freedom was under threat and it was therefore an advantage to the peasantry to have the "feudal ties" terminated. But there was already a rising peasant class and a nobility with its position undermined politically and financially. The peasants were favoured financially in that land tax assessments were reviewed in conjunction with the implementation of the military allotment system to ensure the future buoyancy of the farmsteads. But the taxes *were* then to be paid; the officers had to draw their allotted income and could not agree to remissions as the nobility had often done. Moreover – and more importantly – the unfavourable trend in farm prices continued until the end of the century.

Within the nobility, the groups were many. Heckscher's observations may appear reasonable but they are often rather freely outlined. In general he underestimates the losses of manors and the farmsteads belonging to them. But it is true that even the hardest-hit of the nobility showed a remarkable ability to preserve their landed estates, including those affected by both the reduction and the inquiry into the regency. The ways were many. Heckscher mentions advantageous marriages and survival of manors as dwellings allotted to officers or subject to an obligation to furnish cavalrymen. But there was much more: the opportunities offered by the high salaries of the old nobility to acquire or save manors; leasing of repossessed manors – this also happened within Sweden; enfeoffment in repossessed estates, and favourable agreements with the Crown. It was by such means that one of the most prominent figures of the period, Johan Gabriel Stenbock, avoided the unpleasant consequences of the regency inquiry.

The class that was to play the most important part in the future was the new civil servant class, which arose as a result of the salary reforms and the huge transfer of land and revenues from the nobility via the Crown to officers and bureaucrats, both nobles and commoners. The revenues from landed estates, too, now became a salary that followed the post, not the person. It is within this class that we find the leading supporters of the new regime.

The wealthy burgher class, on the other hand, existed already, and its members had been associated with or were themselves among the revenue collectors. It now suffered from the partial national bankruptcy that followed close after the commissions of inquiry. In the new military state it was no longer so necessary to ensure the availability of credit. Creditors were therefore dealt with harshly and their claims were beaten down or rejected altogether. The same treatment was meted out to those to whom landed estates had been sold or pledged against claims, who now frequently lost them. The revenue collectors who had granted credit were particularly unfortunate, among them Joel Gripenstierna, who was declared to owe the Crown 1,154,296 *daler* whereas he considered that he had a claim of 3,377,825 *daler* against the Crown! Behind him and others in the same situation were whole consortia who were dragged into the muddle. In other respects, too, the new regime asserted its interests at the expense of financiers and burghers. Like others, they had in their extraordinary taxes to pay one-fourth of the return on all "productive capital". To large-scale merchants and businessmen this type of taxation must have been particularly unfortunate. It would have been surprising if they had not, like Johan Gabriel Stenbock, transferred their assets abroad.

In these circumstances, it is difficult to describe the policies adopted under absolutism as favourable to the bourgeoisie. In this respect the situation was different under the new Danish absolutism, which was much more accommodating, e.g. in the settlement of debts which took place after the upheaval of 1660 and largely took the form of selling landed estates to creditors.

It was, on the other hand, a highly militarized society that now emerged. The newly obtained resources had almost all gone to the armed forces, which on account of the allotment system and the rural provision of soldiers and seamen had a strangely agrarian look about it. Perhaps the aspect that is most characteristic of Sweden and the system is that new groups now take root in the countryside and remain there for a long time. One such group, cavalrymen, soldiers and seamen, existed before but now received definitive remuneration in the cottages which were allotted to them. The other consists of the officers in their allotted dwellings, who along with clergymen, merchants and other new landowners henceforth form an increasingly significant intermediate group. It is now, too, that a pattern of habitation is developed that has left its mark on the Swedish countryside, a pattern that harks back to the plans of officers' dwellings and parsonages that were drawn during this period.

By comparison with developments elsewhere in Europe, Swedish absolutism comes late. But it could hardly have come any sooner: in the forty years between the death of Gustav Adolf and Karl XI's attainment of his majority we have only two short periods of rule by a monarch who has come of age, those of Christina and Karl Gustav. Both attempted to assert the royal power, but neither reached the position of Gustav Adolf during the later years of his rule. The new regency which came to power after the death of Karl Gustav still ruled in accordance with the instrument of government of 1634. Like Christina's regency, it had groups opposing it, not only among the commoners but now also in the nobility and the council of the realm.

At this time, monarchic power was in the ascendant everywhere, and the ideas of its protagonists, such as Hobbes and Pufendorf, reached Sweden by many channels. One route was through Erik Lindeman, ennobled

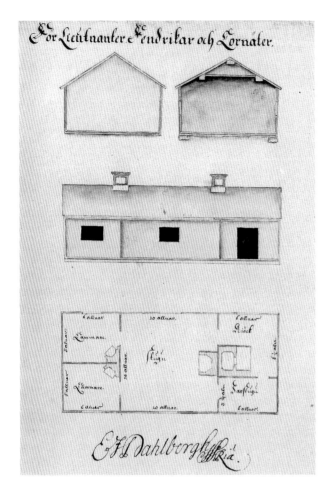

Drawing by Erik Dahlbergh, 1687, of dwelling for "Lieutenants, Ensigns and Cornets". The log cabin had a low turf roof and small panes of glass in the windows. It consisted of an entrance hall and kitchen (right), parlour (centre) and two smaller rooms (left). The dimensions were 10 x 22 ells, i.e. approx. 6 x 13 metres (20 x 42 ft). Photo: The Royal Military Record office.

as Lindschöld and later president of a legal review commission, a count and one of Karl XI's leading advisers. He was familiar with Pufendorf and had translated *Argenis*, a political novel which advocated a powerful monarchy and was a part of the educational programme of the future Karl XII.

So the new ideas were waiting. When they coincided with military disaster, for which the regency was held responsible and in which the young king was seen as a saviour, the road was signposted to absolutism. This was formally established by a series of clarificatory declarations that transferred the various areas of political authority to the king. They were crowned in 1693 by the well-known declaration of the principle of sovereignty, stating that the king (and his descendants) had been instated as "an absolute, sovereign king, whose commands are binding upon all, and who is responsible to no one on earth for his actions but has the power and might at his pleasure as a Christian king to rule and govern his kingdom". At about the same time the court painter Ehrenstrahl produced his allegory of Karl XI's declaration of majority, in which, it has been pointed out, he has Svecia appear in "almost crawling subservience".

The attitude says something about the mood of the time. It already prevailed before 1680 and partly explains the uncompromising actions of the king's men. The same stance was taken in the introduction of absolutism. In the very first of the clarifications, in 1680, it was stated that the king was not bound by any instrument of government but only by the law of Sweden, that the power of decision in the matters he referred to the council of the realm was his alone and that the council was not in any way an intermediary between the king and the people. This was emphatically repeated in the Annulment Act of 1689, by which a series of injurious pronouncements and decisions were repudiated, including those on the validity of the instrument of government of 1634 and the special status of the council of the realm.

The measures were logical. The instrument of

Allegory of the accession to the throne of Karl XI. Painting by D.K. Ehrenstrahl. Drottning-holm Palace.
Photo: The National Swedish Art Museums.

Karl XI and his family. The central figure is Karl X Gustav's queen, Hedvig Eleonora. To the extreme left is Karl XI, next to him the queen dowager. The two children are, from the left, Prince Karl (the future Karl XII) and his sister Hedvig Sofia. Queen Ulrika Eleonora is on the far right. Behind the children Maria Eufrosyne, Karl XI's aunt. Above the family group hangs a portrait of Karl X Gustav. Portrait by D.K. Ehrenstrahl, 1683. Gripsholm Palace.
Photo: The National Swedish Art Museums.

government had created an alternative to the personal rule of the king and filled an important role during the exercise of power by the regencies. Previous monarchs had to some extent interfered with its workings, but in its essentials it had survived as the system of administration and also to a great degree as the system of government. Until now, when acceptance of absolutism placed all power in the hands of the king.

Significantly, Karl XI found it necessary also to remould his administration. The older government offices were divested of large areas of duty, which were made the responsibility of the king's representatives. In addition there were all the new commissions to supervise reduction, inquiry and military allotment. At the same time the functions of the high officers of state and the councillors of the realm were taken over by presidents of government offices and privy councillors. Many of these were new men, others were from the old nobility. In their relationship to the king, there was no difference between them; the degree of dependency was the same.

Control of the country as a whole also tightened. The reduction and the military allotment system made it necessary to carry out a full-scale inventory of all farms and their revenues, an inventory which led in many cases to a review of the assessment units allocated. This control also included population statistics and, as before, was exercised primarily by the clergy, through both their general care and their parish rolls, which were now extended. In Gustav Adolf's time they had had to keep registers of personal taxation and conscription and, to ensure that these could be kept accurate, lists of births and deaths as well. The requirement continued after these levies had been reimposed on the farms, and was written into the Church Regulation Art of 1686 as a part of the official duties of the clergy. They were to keep registers of births, marriages and deaths, of catechetical meetings, and now also of change of domicile. The latter had first been demanded by Gustav Adolf, but it was only with absolutism that it was put into effect. Such a register was also essential to the total registration of the

Register of catechetical meetings or household examinations from Björkskog Parish 1688–1710, containing information about all families including all persons in the household. The dates at the top of the page are the dates of parish catechetical meetings and the columns give details of place of birth, age, ability to read and knowledge of the catechism, prayers, confession etc.
Rååbyy, croft
Anders Eek, soldier, born i Odensvi(?), 40 years old.
Wife Karin Hansd(otter), born in Eker, 42 years old.
Mother-in-law, Anna, born in Barkarö, 86 years old, died 1692.
Also … Brita Eriksdotter, born in Närke, 42 years old.
Children
Päder Andersson … 1695, born i Björskog, 9 years old, died 1699.
Anna Andersdotter, born in Björskog, 8 years old, died 1696 …
Jonas Andersson, soldier, born in Kolbäck, 26 years old, killed in the Battle Narva against the Russians November 1700.

Register of persons moving into or out of the parish of By, 1688–1700.

Persons arriving in the parish from January 1, 1688.

No. 1 *Lars Hansson with his wife Karin Eriksdotter from Nora Vicarage with the certificate of approval of Rev. Elias Noraeus, dated January 17, 1688, presented January 29, 1688. Living at Strandmon.*

No. 3 *the son of Erik Svensson of Bagghyttan, employed in Garpenberg for 1 year, came with the certificate of Rev. Peder Vagnström, dated June 15, 1688.*

population. For this is what it was; with homestead taxes and the rural provision of soldiery a registration system for purely fiscal reasons was not as important as it had been.

As before, the instruments of royal power now emerge as the military, the administration and the Church. But there are now certain changes in their relationship to the sovereign. During the time of Gustav Adolf the army and navy and the administration bore the stamp of the nobility and reflected its relationship with the king, a relationship that allowed an appreciable degree of autonomy, at least for the leading men in the administration. Here there was a feudal element, as there was in the donation of landed property, often more important than the actual salary, with which services were rewarded. But during the period of autocracy we find other, newer conditions of employment. The gratuities are no longer a part of the picture, reward is in the form of salaries which are properly paid out or collected from those liable to tax. It is this secure salary situation, rather than a survival of the feudal structure, that explains the loyalty of the civil servants – and the nobility – to the absolute monarchy.

As a result of this, the attitude to public service seems also to have changed. The semi-independent magnates had disappeared, those who in return for their benefices were prepared to commit themselves to projects which involved them in expenditure and who did not count too heavily on their formal salaries. One of the last of these was the king's leading adviser, Johan Gyllenstierna, who ruined himself with an embassy to Denmark in 1680. After the reduction and the inquiry into the regency this sort of thing was no longer possible, and the benefices had now gone.

In the case of the clergy, there is greater continuity. As we have seen, the monarch still found the clergy useful for their preaching to and control of his subjects, and in this respect he now made greater demands of them. In keeping with their theocratic view of the state, they were also prepared to serve those in power. But they hesitated when the authorities intervened in areas that were the Church's own. This was where conflict had arisen before, in particular when Gustav Adolf and Axel Oxenstierna had tried to establish a Church supervisory board with secular features. Karl XI went further and nominated a lay commission to review the proposed new organization of the Church, which had long been in preparation, and then drew up the Church Regulation Act himself, presenting it to the clergy as a *fait accompli* at the *riksdag* of 1686. That there was opposition here and elsewhere is well-known, but how widespread it was is difficult to ascertain – the matters concerned were sensitive.

The same may be said of the reaction in general. The interests that were favoured by absolutism can more or less be identified, but how it stood in public opinion is harder to assess. This is inevitable with a regime that did not tolerate dissenting voices. Admittedly the *riksdag* continued, but its function was little more than that of a rubber stamp. However, it was to the *riksdag* that the different Estates of the realm still made their complaints, and these say a good deal about the things that provoked a definite reaction. The same applies to the individual petitions that could be lodged with authorities of various levels of competence. They usually relate to the many changes brought about by the implementation of the military allotment system and the local maintenance of soldiery, and the fiscal questions that these involved. And these petitions were also of importance to the monarch as a necessary source of information and as a safety valve for discontent.

The New War and the Long Epilogue

By the middle of the 1690s the work of military organization was almost complete. The army, the navy and the fortifications were all newly constructed, well equipped and tested under Karl XI's supervision. The experiences gained in the wars of the 1670s served as a guide: as always, attempts were made to correct previous miscalculations and guard against previous blunders.

The implications of this were also obvious at the time. This is evident from a book which appeared in 1694 entitled *An Account of Sweden: together with an Extract of the History of that Kingdom*. The author was presumably the English Stockholm diplomat, John Robinson. Whether he wrote the whole book is uncertain but he seems at least to have been responsible for the section on the Swedish armed forces, which is strikingly well informed and filled with respect for the military reforms. Only with the introduction of absolutism, says Robinson, has it been possible to deal with the weaknesses of the former system. Now, however, the country has an army that is ready for action and can be mobilized at short notice.

This was demonstrated a few years after Karl XI's death, when Sweden's neighbours decided the time was ripe for attack. The mobilization that took place in 1700 was very different from those that had gone before, such as that of 1655, which has been described as "starting a war with no money". Now there was a national army, ready to take the field, and money for recruiting reinforcements. Everything had been prepared, including alternative deployment plans, supplies and financial reserves. Moreover the *riksdag* had given Karl XI the right to levy both war contributions and taxes in kind for the deployment of the troops. Altogether, it was the answer to a general staff's prayer. In the plan that was implemented, the route of every single company was specified, as were the places where they were to be marshalled in larger units.

The build-up to the war and the events that followed have been the subject of many descriptions, both literary and scholarly. Scarcely any stage of Swedish history can have been so often discussed as this, nor so hotly debated. The controversy has centred chiefly on the central figure in the drama, Karl XII, who until his death in 1718 was incontestably in charge of both policy and war.

What we lack to an unusual degree from Karl XII is material which might throw light on the motives for his actions. As an absolute monarch he did not leave much such evidence, certainly not at the times when he was in the field and made his decisions after reports had been presented by secretaries at his field headquarters. Historians have therefore for the most part had to judge him by his actions, and often they have been either highly critical of Karl XII or tried to explain and vindicate him. In the latter case they have not infrequently tried so diligently to justify his actions as to end up by portraying him as both a far-sighted politician and a military commander by divine right.

If Axel Oxenstierna had been asked to judge, he would undoubtedly have seen Karl XII as one of the foolish monarchs whom he wanted to circumscribe with his instrument of government. Without it, he believed, they would bring the kingdom down. The kingdom did indeed fall, although it took nineteen long years, filled with war against, finally, no less than five hostile states. The puzzle is not really the final disasters but the fact that the country could survive for so long in its increasingly exposed and desperate situation. The only possible explanation lies in the system of the military state, a system whose efficiency had been steadily improved under absolutism, but one whose foundations had been laid by Axel Oxenstierna, even though his model was not the one finally chosen.

Historians have concentrated their attention on the financial side of the problem, i.e. on the military allotment system that was the chosen solution. Eli Heckscher, whom I have mentioned, was always critical of all forms of state regulation and considered that the military allotment system's rigid methods of payment in kind did not work in wartime and nor did the military organization in general. Reduction and commissions of inquiry had also cut off the supply of credit, which could not by any means be replaced by the reserves accumulated by Karl XI. To this interpretation Fredrik Lagerroth objected – in the 1930s – that the rearrangements resulting from the war had been foreseen and that the financing system had not had the rigid character Heckscher imagined.

The discussion between these two was conducted on quite a general level, without any real confrontation with the source material. A more recent study of the way in which mobilization was carried out shows that it was able to take place within the framework of Karl XI's reforms and with the aid of only limited domestic loans. If we examine the continued financing of the war we find that the borrowing was usually adequate: as been pointed out earlier, credit did not play such an important part in the new system. But the troops were maintained mainly with what could still be extracted from the battlegrounds and also with funds that were now more readily available at home than before.

The main problem, however, was the manpower that was needed in order to replace losses, which were still very high. Remarkably enough, it proved possible to stretch the original agreements to lay this burden, too, on the military allotment system, sometimes in forms that constituted a singular hybrid between conscription and militia.

That this was possible was due to the firm grip which absolutism still had on the country and the control that the king was able to exercise even when he was in the field. During his years in Turkey, however, some strain did begin to develop in contact between him and the council at home, which was now ordered to deliver a new army to replace the one defeated in Russia. It was to be taken across the Baltic and meet the king as he returned home through Poland. When it finally set off in 1712 under the command of Magnus Stenbock, however, it was surrounded by superior enemy forces and obliged instead to make for Danmark, where it eventually capitulated in 1713.

Nevertheless, in the late autumn of 1714 Karl XII was back in Pomerania, and the next year he was in Sweden. He then set about remodelling both the administration and the taxation system in order to permit an even more efficient use of the country's resources. His assistants were new men, in particular the Holsteiner Georg Heinrich von Görtz, and the council and the administrative heads were pushed aside. This in turn deepened the gulf between the king and the higher ranks of the bu-

The many portraits of Karl XII – with the exception of those from his youth – depart from cinventional practice in depicting him in austerely simple uniform. Portrait by J.H. Wedekind, 1719. Gripsholm Palace.
Photo: The National Swedish Art Museums.

reaucracy. In other ways, too, relations with the social groups that supported absolutism had become strained. The heavy contributions and the salary cuts that were now renewed annoyed the civil servants, and the officers began to feel the competition for dwellings which, under the new system, had taken the place of donations of land. There were not enough to go round, as the number of officers had risen quickly during the war, and not all of them could now be provided for within Sweden. When peace came, the problem would be acute, a new variation of the problem of demobilization.

Despite these difficulties, Karl XII succeeded in raising new armies and new resources from his empire, which now consisted only of Sweden itself, and for as long as he lived he was able to maintain his military dictatorship. Only the shot at Fredrikshald in 1718 – from wherever it came – cleared the way for a change. That the already precarious absolutism had to fall was obvious; there was no longer any group in the community that could be expected to support it. Great-power status had been preserved in previous times of crisis, but on this occasion large parts of the empire were occupied and – perhaps most important of all – there was in Europe at that time no significant power whose own interest lay in maintaining Sweden's ascendancy. France was greatly weakened after her own wars, and England was more likely to benefit – commercially – from being able to establish direct contact with the Russia that was now pushing forward to the Baltic.

So imperial Sweden had to fall. With it disappeared the Swedish military state in its then form, a form in which military demands had been allowed also to determine the structure of the state itself and the allocation of resources, and thus played a decisive part in the sweeping social changes that are characteristic of Sweden in the seventeenth century.

References

This essay is based on a number of recent essays in which I discuss, in a synthesizing form, the Swedish military state of the seventeenth century and its political system. See:

Nilsson, S.A., ”Militärstaten i funktion”, in *Gustav II Adolf – 350 år efter Lützen* (1982).

– ”Den karolinska militärstaten”, in *Tre Karlar* (1984).

– ”1634 års regeringsform i det svenska statssystemet”, *Statsvetenskaplig tidskrift* 1984.

For other literature, the reader is referred to the bibliographies accompanying these essays.

See in addition:

Attman, A., *The struggle for Baltic markets. Powers in conflict, 1558–1618* (1979).

Lindegren, J., ”The Swedish Military State, 1560–1720”, *Scandinavian Journal of History* 1985.

Lundkvist, S., ”Säkerhet och fred. Kring den westfaliska fredens problematik”, in *Utrikespolitik och historia. Studier tillägnade Wilhelm Carlgren* (1987).

Roberts, M. et al, *Sweden's age of greatness, 1632–1718* (1973).

Roberts, M., *The Swedish imperial experience, 1560–1718* (1979).

Frontispiece to Stiernhielm's poem Hercules. *Royal Swedish Library.*
Photo: Royal Swedish Library.

Visual Culture in Seventeenth-Century Sweden
Images of Power and Knowledge

ALLAN ELLENIUS

In 1658, Georg Stiernhielm, poet, natural philosopher and antiquarian published his famous poem "Hercules", written in classical hexameters. Its copperplate frontispiece shows the hero of antiquity faced with the choice between Lady Virtue and Lady Lust; in verse of copious fluency we follow his trial by all manner of worldly temptations. When Lady Virtue has completed her plea, the poem is suddenly at an end and the reader is left to decide for himself between the two ways of life. It goes without saying that he should travel the road towards the temple of honour that once was the dream of Hercules.

The poem of Hercules at the crossroads is a part of the outpouring of newly awakened cultural enthusiasm that was characteristic of the reign of Queen Christina. It not only confirms that a Renaissance concept of virtue has taken root in Swedish soil. It also served excellently as a memorandum for the new generation of nobility who had felt the fresh breezes blowing through the court of Queen Christina and who had perhaps, at the University of Uppsala, listened to or even orated on the great paragons of virtue from antiquity, so eloquently portrayed by Roman authors. In the concept of *virtus* was concentrated much of the optimism and affirmation of life that are indissolubly linked with the Renaissance. Here was an intellectual core that to the most influential Estate of the realm could be combined with heroic exploits on the field of battle – to illustrate the qualities expected in the ideal prince and aristocrat, the art of emblematics used the Roman emperor, standing on top of the globe with book in one hand and sword in the other. For the young great power this was an inspiring combination; the newly attained position needed to be paraded to the world with visual and architectural symbols of the greatest cogency. Summoning up existing pictorial ideas of high moral and artistic value, Sweden became a part of the mainstream of European Culture as it had not been since the late Middle Ages.

These ambitions could not be realized without assistance from abroad. Just as scholarship was advanced by foreign university professors coming into Sweden, so artists and eminent architects were recruited to carry out the commissions. Aesthetic culture became an essential part of the face that the country presented to the world.

Political virtues

The art of the Swedes and the way they shaped their physical surroundings thus came to an appreciable extent to reflect their desire to express the new awareness of power. Imagery indicative of the new attitude is that which took shape on the royal ship "Wasa", which sank in 1628 but is now well-known thanks to the research work of marine archaeologists. The wealth of carvings and ornamentation constituted a visual statement whose clear reference point was in the defender of the faith and war hero Gustav II Adolf. The concepts of humanism and also of the Old Testament and of Gothic antiquity were invoked to emphasize his decisive role. The ship was to cleave the waves with the same triumphant power as the Old Testament multitudes when they annihilated the enemy under commanders such as Gideon, David and Judas Maccabaeus. The idea is fully in harmony with Gustav Adolf's soldiery ordinance, which

The stern of the warship
Wasa. *Reconstruction*
of the stern by Björn
Landström.
Photo: The Swedish
National Maritime
Museum.

has been analysed by Sven A. Nilsson from a different angle in his contribution to this volume, and which cites examples from both the Bible and classical antiquity. When the king fell on the battlefield of Lützen in 1632, elegiac tribute was paid to him as the new Hercules who had won honour with his victories in Germany: the hero of antiquity is also among the figures decorating the ship, here simply an illustration of the fact that the classical philosophy of virtue was becoming embedded in the intellectual consciousness of the age. Wholly in keeping with the theme, the rudder of the ship was adorned with the Swedish lion, on the point of crushing the enemy.

Visual representation could therefore be a most striking expression of hope, while also serving as an instrument of propaganda. As Sweden enters the war in Germany, Gustav Adolf becomes an important part of the flow of propagandizing images; the psychomachy of the Middle Ages – the conflict between vice and virtue – is renewed here as a struggle between the Protestant faith and the papal Church. In mass-produced copperplate engravings the political pamphlets acquire pictorial form. The theme is unequivocal: the Swedish king is seen as the instrument of God, he is the Lion of the North (*der Löwe aus der Mitternacht*), discharging his historical mission. On one of the sheets, Gustav Adolf is depicted as the Christian soldier *Miles Christianus*, successfully repulsing the onslaughts of the Devil, on another he is Hercules, in victorious combat with the apocalyptic monster of the Catholic Church, while elsewhere he rides forward in his triumphal carriage, surrounded by a host of virtues. There is certainly no shortage of arresting details in this crowding imagery.

The imagery of naval architecture and propaganda recurs in the monumental buildings that were erected in Stockholm and out on the country estates. In the capital, a remarkable status-consciousness is attested by the new Palace of the Nobility, conceived in mid-century and designed by the Dutch architect Jost Vingboons in Palladian style but crowned with a two-tiered manor roof executed in something close to native tradition.

The building functions as a conscious system of symbols, from the choice of style to the sculptural embellishment and the gilded inscription on the frieze. The chancellor, Axel Oxenstierna, was firmly of the opinion that the palace ought to be Italianate in character and Klas Fleming, the head of the committee in charge of the project, argued that it had to have a magnificence that would ensure its renown. The building is also distinguished for the less typical care that went into its planning. The original plans, drawn by Simon De la Vallée, who had been brought from France for the purpose, envisaged spacious courtyards, but after these had been trimmed to a single block, the building came to appear as a distillation of the ideas we have already encountered in the myth of Hercules. Above one of the portals is the inscription *Arte et Marte*, with reliefs on either side alluding both to war and to the literary virtues. Hercules himself appears in the roof area with his club and accompanied by an inscription indicating the way through the labours to the distant prize of honour. In a central position, dominating the main facade, parades the Estate of the nobility, flanked by Bravery and Study (cultivation), while the Roman majuscules of the inscription stress the importance of the forefathers' glorious example. Among the decoration on the roof there is also an altar to the native land – the cult of virtue was inseparably bound up with patriotic conceptions.

The expansive ambitions of the nobility are also reflected in the interior of the palace. In the great hall, the walls of which are adorned with the escutcheons of the noble families, the painted ceiling is an apotheosis of the young great power. It is the work of Karl XI's court painter, David Klöcker Ehrenstrahl, and dates from 1674. Ehrenstrahl had come from Germany to Sweden in the service of the returning Field Marshal Carl Gustaf Wrangel, and after studies in Italy in the 1650s he had embarked on a successful career at the Caroline court, of which more will be said. The painting in the Palace of Nobility was a commission wholly in tune with his fervent ambition to use his talent in the glorification of the nation. In the Rome of the High Baroque period he

The Palace of the Nobility.
Photo: Gösta Glase

had seen and evidently strongly admired the breathtaking ceiling of the Palazzo Barberini, painted in the 1630s by Pietro da Cortona, whose divine Providence is crowned with the stellar garland of Eternity and surrounded by a series of scenes from classical mythology. In Stockholm, the central figure is replaced by Svecia, the personification of Sweden, presiding over an assembly of virtues who have gathered in consultation – an allusion to the wise decisions that it was assumed would be reached in the meetings of the *riksdag* in the hall. Unlike the Roman source of his inspiration, the painter executed his huge composition in oils; at the same time he had the heraldic bees of the Barberinis transformed into the national emblem of the three crowns. Fame supplies a musical background, sounding the praises of the young great power on her trumpet.

The power consciousness of the Swedish nobility had developed gradually. Earldoms and baronies had been created back in the sixteenth century, although at the time the glory surrounding those titles was not yet reflected in ostentatious building. It is only with the advent of the Age of Greatness and the enormous growth in wealth that status consciousness swells to the point of demanding architectural settings to compete in magnificence with foreign counterparts. The importance of a political balance of power between the Crown and the aristocracy of the councils was emphasized in several ways and also found expression in the visual arts. When the eminent diplomat Schering Rosenhane was in Germany for the negotiations which resulted in the Treaty of Westphalia, he compiled a collection of emblems entitled *Hortus Regius* and dedicated it to Queen Christina. Like many of his fellow nobles, Rosenhane was quite at home with pictorial symbolism and its uses in expressing moral philosophy and political convictions. In one of the illustrations he has the artist show a building symbolizing Swedish society: the different storeys are represented by the hierarchy of the Estates, with the Estate of the peasants at the bottom and the nobility at the top beneath the royal crown. Scales bearing the crown and the emblems of the re-

Detail of Palace with the inscription Arte et Marte *(by Art and War) above one of the portals.*
Photo: Gösta Clase

A building symbolizing Swedish society. From Hortus Regius,
by Schering Rosenhane. Royal Swedish Library.
Photo: Royal Swedish Library.

spective Estates are in equilibrium and a sceptre that is
seen attached to the four links of a chain underlines the
significance of the inscription, which states that order is
destroyed if balance is disturbed. Schering is, in other
words, making a plea for constitutionalism as a political
system. In the increase in the power of the nobility, the
political position was of vital importance; after their

privileges had been eroded and the reduction (repossess-
sion of landed estates by the Crown) had begun, the
nobles were no longer able to put into effect the ideas
that in the Palace of the Nobility were given such re-
splendent form.

The leading landed magnate and patron of the arts
was Count Magnus Gabriel De la Gardie. Unlike his

father and grandfather, illustrious military commanders, he pursued an administrative career, starting with studies at Uppsala and a lavish embassy to Paris in the 1640s. In a double portrait of 1652 he appears with his consort, Countess Palatine Maria Euphrosyne. They are strolling across a veranda, the count decorously holding the hand of his consort while starting to descend the steps ahead of her. Flowers on the balustrades symbolize love and fertility, the latter also being expressed in the bean pod which the countess is holding in her hand, while a white lapdog serves as a symbol of the woman's marital fidelity. The low angle from which the portrait is painted reinforces its representative character, strongly brought out also by the splendid attire. The painting is the work of the Dutch artist Hendrick Munnichhoven and his *tour de force*. He has sympathetically reproduced the count's taste for luxury and splendour, the *honnête homme* ideal of the new age, which has now begun to compete with the rounded nobleman bequeathed by the Renaissance in Castiglione's famous tract *Il cortegiano*. But the portrait gives only the brilliant exterior of De la Gardie's personality, the role he wished to play on the political stage. In order to scratch below the surface it is necessary to visit him in his own surroundings and there see how with the aid of the visual arts he was able to convey an attitude to life more complex in its nature.

Between Uppsala and Stockholm stands Venngarn, the manor house to which De la Gardie devoted most of his attentions, starting in the 1650s when he had the architect Jean De la Vallée extend it with a pair of projecting wings and a monumental staircase. In addition the building was provided with spacious gardens, among the finest in the country. On the verandas which in those days overlooked the *cour d'honneur* were enthroned sculptures of the Christian virtues, giving an intimation of the imagery unfolding within. Here the four cardinal virtues bore witness to the hold exerted on the popular imagination by the philosophy of Stoicism. From the heights of Baroque illusionism the didactic message could be scaled down to experiences at very close range, as in the numerous emblematic paintings with their succinct maxims. Like Schering Rosenhane, De la Gardie obviously had a feeling for the enigmatic image and its capacity for illuminating the great questions of life for the initiated. Here we meet a polarity which is typical of the Swedish Age of Greatness: the terms of temporal power no longer have any unquestioned authority – they are portrayed now from a timeless perspective, with a marshalling of symbols which suggests the admonishing medieval images of the wheel of life and fortune. The peasant ploughs his fields, the flowers wither and die, the moon runs its courses, all is subject to the law of change. The variations on the theme of the way of life and the voyage of life are endless: the pilgrim sees the vision of Jerusalem, the seafarer is menaced by storms and rocky coasts but then miraculously saved by Christian hope. Reality and the metaphysical mix – the vulnerability of man's existence is contrasted with a confidence in eternal salvation. At times the pictures assume the character of an invocation, a kind of vision of deliverance from torment and wordly temptation. To De la Gardie these were very real experiences, confirmed by contemporary observers: they increased with age and adversity. In religious meditation he found moments of release from what he called "the servitude and vexations of political life".

The mansions of the nobility were laid out to a strictly symmetrical plan, inspired by Italian and French models. The same system is typical of the gardens and their parterres, greenhouses, fountains and sculptures. Exotic plants could be seen in the hothouses, elegant walks led to grottoes and summerhouses. The unrelenting symmetry and axiality of the gardens were more than just an imported fashion, they were a means of subduing chaos; beyond their ordered world, the wilderness was a near neighbour of the manorial estate. In this way they may be seen as a product of power consciousness: nature herself is tamed and compelled to bring tribute to the lord of the manor. A literary genre took shape, which eulogized the splendour of the gardens as a manifestation of the owner's lofty tempera-

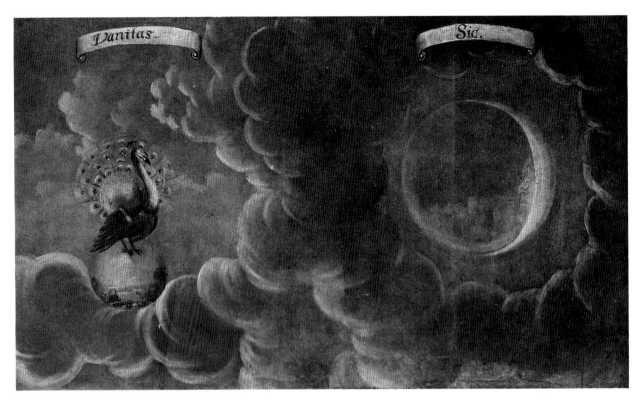

Emblematic painting in the chapel of Venngarn.
Photo: Olle Lindman

ment – an example is provided by the lengthy poem in Latin which the Uppsala professor and national historiographer Johannes Loccenius wrote on the remarkable things to be seen on another estate owned by De la Gardie, Jakobsdal. On a vaster scale, the gardens of Versailles had a similar function, their size and mythological allusions a constant reference to the absolute monarchy.

An echo of life out in the country gardens is to be found in portraiture, particularly in the portrayal of wo-men, which had emerged in the middle of the century from the stylized forms of late Mannerism and now, under the influence of Anthon van Dyck, introduced movement and a kind of romanticizing sentimentality into the characterization of the subject. In David Beck's portrait of Queen Christina, painted in 1650, the new ideal is fully developed. One has the impression that the queen has been strolling in a park and has paused for a moment, with her veil blowing out over her shoulder

Queen Christina. Painting by David Beck, 1650. National Museum of Fine Arts. Photo: The National Swedish Art Museums.

Axel Oxenstierna's chapel in Jäder Church. From Svecia antiqua et hodierna. *Royal Swedish Library.*
Photo: Royal Swedish Library.

and a mood of eventide settling on the landscape in the background. The theme is varied by Ehrenstrahl in his portrait of Ingeborg Banér in the 1660s, in which the park with its climbing plants and the water streaming from the cliffs glimpsed in the background has a suggestion of the Tivoli gardens. Symbolic features also find their way into the actual subjects – in Beck's painting we find that the queen is wearing orange blossom in her hair, an allusion to her wisdom, while in Munnichhoven's portrait of Elisabeth von Königsmark (ca. 1654) the young girl is picking a rose as a reminder of the transience of youthful beauty and in harmony with the atmosphere of melancholy pervading the portrait. In each case there is a new concept of womanhood, inspired by the *courtoisie* which was increasingly current in fashionable circles.

Among these noble milieus must also be considered the memorial chapels, which begin to appear at churches near to the country seats after the death of Gustav Adolf and the building of his *conditorium* at Riddarholm Church in Stockholm. These monuments are a good barometer of the nobility's aspirations to power, presenting a symbolism that to a considerable degree commemorates worldly achievements but which naturally also puts them in a larger perspective. In the chapel of Field Marshal Lars Kagg at Floda Church, Stiernhielm has composed an inscription that joins with the classical allegories of the ornamentation to pronounce that the road to heaven is also the road of virtue. As at the Palace of the Nobility, we find such qualities as Strength and Glory, which transform the memorial chapel into a setting for a humanist cult of honour. In some cases the whole church tended to be annexed as a monument to the dead nobleman, as occurred at Jäder, where Chancellor Axel Oxenstierna had the church lengthened with a new chancel at the east end and installed his own memorial chapel beneath it. In many cases the walls and ceiling were adorned with stuccowork, as, for example, at Skokloster, where they showed the military exploits of General Herman Wrangel, depicting him on horseback but also asleep on the tomb awaiting the resurrection being proclaimed by trumpeting angels in the vault. At the front of the chancel of the church at Österhaninge stands a monument to Admiral of the Realm Klas Bielkenstierna, with sculptured groups of trophies, portraits and Father Time as prominent features. Everybody in the church was confronted with this monument to martial honour; in the chancel or on the walls hung the ancestral arms and the standard which had been used in the funeral ceremony and whose function was to give emphatic legitimacy to the nobility's claim to power. Funereal pomp gradually assumed such forms that it had to be checked by ordinances; indeed, Axel Oxenstierna himself urged moderation when he laid down the programme for his own funeral. Like that of De la Gardie, his life had two sides: he, too, was familiar with the world of prayer and meditation and of private converse with God. It was a world far removed from the nationalistic displays of glitter and magnificence that went with the task of representing Estate and country.

Triumph of the Dynasty

Thus, with appropriate selection from the flora of symbols, the visual arts could be used to convey the moods and convictions that formed the ideology of the Age of Greatness. As we have seen, the images were widely disseminated, some being addressed to the exclusive audience of the court and the aristocracy, others circulating among the crews of the warships or in those quarters overseas that were to be swayed by monarchic and Lutheran propaganda. To a large extent, it is an art coloured by literature; its penetrative force was due to the origin of the images in mythological, historical and religious concepts. The branches of the arts meet in fruitful symbiosis – literary figures occur in sculpture and painting and can also be seen on the stage in the extravagant court theatricals that were for a time an important part of the panegyric art. Here they appeared with the speeches and gestures that the observer of the sculptures and pictures had to conjure up in his own imagination.

Court festivities had received a boost in the reign of Christina, when the court in Stockholm was the scene of ballet and drama. The queen herself would take part and was hailed as the new Minerva, patroness of the arts and learning and a lover of peace. Justitia, Prudentia and Pax appeared on stage and gave tangible form to the political message. Triumphal carriages displayed Fortuna as a felicitous symbol of success in battle and the happy state of the realm, a reminder that Gustav Adolf had been hailed in his triumph as Augustus, the new prince of peace. The coronation ceremony of 1650 was also graced with allegorical elements; De la Gardie, still in favour at Queen Christina's court, donated for the occasion the "silver throne", the magnificent ceremonial seat which bore, along with the embellishments of state heraldry, sculptures of Justice and Wisdom, the virtues which should be the outstanding characteristics of a regal personage. Together with Peace, moreover, they had a long lineage in the imagery of jurisprudence as it appears in the frontispieces of editions of the law.

Court pageantry with allegorical features continued into the Caroline era. Attention was paid to the moral education of the young Karl XI at an early age, as, for instance, in the ballet *Tugend-Lohn* of 1659, addressed to the king, in which Hercules appears with Virtue and Renown. Ten years later Stiernhielm's "Hercules" was dramatized by the poet Samuel Columbus and an ode to the king was inserted. The same period saw the decoration of one of the most splendid examples of regal glorification in imperial Sweden, the state bedchamber at Drottningholm Palace. In this new palatial setting it seemed natural to continue in the idiom that had been perfected in the literary panegyric.

With the building of Drottningholm, the queen dowager, Hedvig Eleonora, became one of the leading builders and patrons of the arts of the Caroline era. She stands for dynastic continuity, untiringly active until the collapse of Swedish imperialism – she died the year before her grandson Karl XII fell at the fortress of Fredriksten, near Fredrikshald, in 1718. Drottningholm

The state bedchamber at Drottningholm.
Photo: Olle Lindman

Palace, designed by Nicodemus the Elder, is very much a monument to the dynasty. Here in the centre of the symmetrical building are the remarkable staircase hall, and also the guardrooms, the state bedchamber and a gallery decorated with paintings of Karl X Gustav's military achievements. The rooms were also filled with portraits of kinsfolk close and distant, together with allegorical paintings paying homage in various ways to the Caroline dynasty.

The facade towards the garden has a doorway with strict Doric-Tuscan lines, a discreet suggestion of the triumphal arch motif, which is further developed in the gallery just inside, where a monochrome painted ceiling shows a triumphal procession. When the visitor reaches the axially placed staircase, the surroundings strike a different note; the military feats and the portraits of ancient kings of the Goths, so important to national self-promotion, give way to a tribute to the peaceful arts. To climb the staircase is positively to mount Parnassus, already celebrated in Queen Christina's court ballets and displaying here both the nine Muses in various movements and representations of Apollo and Minerva, in other words the same figures as surround Hedvig Eleonora's monogram in Ehrenstrahl's crowning plafond. The ensemble was created by Nicolaes Millich, the leading sculptor of the period in Sweden. In all probability, Minerva was intended to inspire thoughts of the builder herself; it is possible to discern Hedvig Eleonora's features, albeit highly idealized. Around 1670, Karl XI had begun to be acclaimed as Apollo, a stage in the spread from France of the astral symbolism that now becomes an increasingly common feature of the Swedish royal panegyric. A painting by Ehrenstrahl shows the sun god with the facial features of Karl XI, portrayed after slaying the dragon Python. In the staircase hall at Drottningholm Hedvig Eleonora combines the exaltation of the kings of Sweden with a celebration of the arts, a cultural achievement to which laudatory allusion is also made in the illustrations on the vaulting.

The state bedchamber is the most richly decorated room in the palace. Surviving drawings show that it was among the units whose position had been decided from the start. It is approached through two fine French suites, which prepare the visitor for entry. The ornamentation has very personal associations with the dowager queen, and it is likely that it incorporates her express wishes. There was obviously a consistent emphasis on quality: the pilaster architecture and its ornate capitals, the sculptured framework of the ceiling, the rich floor inlays of expensive imported woods (boxwood, cypress, palm, walnut, ebony), the paintings and emblematic tablets set into the ceiling and walls. It was here that the efforts of Hedvig Eleonora's leading artists

and craftsmen converged – not only Tessin but also Carlo Carove, Ehrenstrahl, Millich and Burchard Precht. During the 1660s the intention evidently developed of making the room the vehicle for certain themes reflecting the situation of the dowager queen and the young king. The queen's wishes were implemented by people around her who were experienced in the creation of such settings. Traditional visual concepts and contemporary allusion could now be combined in a supreme unity. As the bedchamber had no practical use (Hedvig Eleonora's own residential suite lay in another part of the palace), it could be designed to function as a state and ceremonial room. The result was a dynastic *sanctuarium*, in which the memory of Karl X Gustav was combined with the hopes resting in the young monarch.

The bedchamber and the dignification of the bed of state with columns and archway motifs bring to mind the contemporary judicial and religious ideas associated with matrimony. In the ceiling area the connubial bond is affirmed in a painting in which divine Providence is enthroned among the clouds above a pair of linked hands. The surrounding emblems contain variations on the theme of the dowager queen's conviction that she will one day be reunited with her departed consort.

The religious undertone of the setting recurs in the portrayal of the life of Karl XI, which begins with a painting on the inner alcove ceiling. The newborn prince is being handed down to the Fates, of whom Clotho is receiving the child. Here the thread of life is being spun that appears in both of the murals. Lachesis is receiving from the king's guardian angel his genius, a series of symbols indicating the disciplines necessary to the king's upbringing. In the final scene of the series the genius is protecting the thread of life from being cut by the scissors of Atropos and allowing it to be drawn up through the ring of stars that symbolizes immortality. The young king's way through life is thus presented as a path of virtue. The inspirational sources lay in Italian and Baroque art, but Ehrenstrahl has produced a personal and seemly modification of the impression he has received from existing ideas. The colour scale is muted to harmonize with the original dark shade of the walls, against which the gilt stood out in heavy splendour.

It may seem remarkable that the young king is to such a high degree represented by his genius, and that he himself is not depicted as in similar series on the Continent. The elevation of the person has become synonymous with an assertion of the sublimity of virtue. The tendency to abstraction becomes more natural when one discovers that the sequence of images in the paintings and emblems has its analogies in the contemporary court theatre.

One of the most engaging figures on the Caroline scene is Erik Lindschöld, count, councillor of the realm and also a poet in the panegyric genre. He was commissioned by Hedvig Eleonora to compose rhyming verses for the ballet *Den stoora Genius*, intended for the birthday of Karl XI on 24 November 1669 and performed by a cast of sixty in the December of the same year. Like Ehrenstrahl's paintings, they describe the life of man; here again there is the introduction of genius, the guardian angel, which guides man's work and will and appeals to his better instincts. On the strength of the good qualities which it represents, the king bids his guardian spirit address his subjects on the duties and characteristics of a good king. The work includes a tribute to Hedvig Eleonora and her care of the young Karl XI, while manhood presents Hercules facing the choice between virtue and vice. The outcome is in no doubt; Fame proclaims the king's glory and the libretto ends in a spirit of boundless faith in the future.

This ballet, with its surely very extensive preliminaries, can hardly have escaped the notice of Ehrenstrahl, who was in continous contact with the court. When in 1670 it was his turn to glorify Karl XI in the figure of Apollo, he worked in the same panegyric register as Lindschöld, now repeated in the latter's long poem of congratulation on the king's next birthday. Painting and literature were a mutual stimulus.

The manner in which Karl XI is portrayed is in many ways typical of the striving to construct a role that could be played in public. The discrepancy between the role and the reality was noticed at the time; the description of the king by the Italian diplomat Lorenzo Magalotti is well known: when he walked through the rooms of the palace he did so as if walking on glass; but on horseback he looked a real king. Karl XI was personally shy and awkward, and he had difficulty in reading and writing. Our picture of him bears the imprint of those around him to a noticeable degree; while advisers from the untitled nobility prepared his way to the role of absolute monarch, so he appeared in art and in courtly pageants stage-managed according to the latest Continental fashion. There is no trace of the diffident youth when he appears at his coronation in 1672 in the *Certamen equestre*, a sumptuous carousel in which the performers were dressed as Goths and Romans. The king himself rides out attired as a military commander in a plumed helmet and bearing the title *Eques gloriae*, knight of Honour. The whole pageant was engraved in copper in Nuremberg from a model drawn by Ehrenstrahl.

With the emergence of the nation-state in the sixteenth century, the demand for a ceremonial ambience in the portrayal of the sovereign had also grown. The state portrait developed into a recognizable genre in Sweden as early as the Vasa period. The intention of conveying a lifelike picture of the facial features merged increasingly with the wish to demonstrate in various ways the high office, which according to the theory of government was conferred by God. During the era of political absolutism this development reached a peak; the highly trained court painter stood ready to execute his orders. In France, Charles Lebrun became the loyal servant of Louis XIV, influential also in the French Academy of Painting and Sculpture. He had his Swedish counterpart in Ehrenstrahl, notwithstanding the absence here of an academy to dictate the direction of artistic life with uncompromising authority.

Ehrenstrahl's grand tour to Italy, France and England had shown him examples of how the princely apotheosis was visualized. He followed them with a theoretical awareness and a versatile adjustment to the varying demands of the patron. The best evidence of his am-

*Self-portrait by D.K.
Ehrenstrahl, 1691.
National Museum of
Fine Arts.
Photo: The National
Swedish Art Museums.*

bition to use his art to the glory of his sovereign may be the self-portrait which he painted in 1691 and which found its place at Drottningholm. According to an inscription on the back of the portrait he wished the picture to show how he "sought from love of the art of painting and his invention [i.e. creative selection of theme] to elevate the immortal reputation of the mighty." The portrait shows him sitting in front of his easel, just about to paint. But he is uncertain of the subject. Then Imagination and Painting come to his aid, the former appearing from the shadowy background with a sheet of paper in her hand on which she declares the celebration of the sovereign to be the true purpose of art. Painting lays a confiding hand on the artist's shoulder and passes him the palette and brushes. The picture tells of an action, and aims at the same time to show that the painter was master of the means of realizing his noble task: the flying Cupid is holding a mask and a chain, the links of which symbolize the different constituents of the completed work of art, from choice of subject and composition to colour, light, shade and movement. He had displayed his ability in the enhancement of his master's renown on the ceiling of the Palace of the Nobility, as in the early allegories at Drottningholm, and during the closing decades of the century he was to provide further proofs of his capacity.

Two paintings, executed as companion pieces in 1674–75, are characteristic. In *Historien och Ryktet* (History and Fame), Ehrenstrahl seeks with his own commentary to remind sovereigns that both their good and their other deeds are subject to the judgment of eternity. *Sanningen och Tiden* (Truth and Time) also covers the common ground of allegory; in contrast to the timeless aspect of the companion painting, this one deals rather with the practical morality of action – with time, the truth will be revealed. In both cases, Ehrenstrahl has created fluid compositions that show his treatment of colour to advantage.

In the early 1680s the court painter produces a painting which is central to the theme of his work and indeed to the panegyric genre as a whole: *Dygdens odödliga belöning* (The Immortal Reward of Virtue). The figure of a man is borne aloft by Virtue, who crowns his head with laurels. Billowing clouds surround the figures, while far below on earth the silhouette of Scandinavia can be made out. The flying mantles are painted with fluid brush strokes which accentuate the interplay of light and shade. From the earth, the movement is upward, towards the flood of light to which the genius of the state bedchamber earlier drew the eye.

Originally the picture hung at the manor of Ulriksdal, near Stockholm, above a door in the royal presence chamber. Even if it was not Ehrenstrahl's intention to allude specifically to the king, a contemporary visitor can surely have had no difficulty in making the link between the content of the painting and the most important person at the audience. The year in which this painting was completed was the year of the *riksdag* that took the decisive steps towards the introduction of absolutism.

Apotheosis is also a central theme of the large group portrait of the royal family that Ehrenstrahl produced in 1683. The family is grouped around a table in a manner somewhat reminiscent of French painting and particularly of the royal portraits of Pierre Mignard. It is a secluded setting, screened in by heavy curtains and with a magnificent oriental carpet on the floor. The portrait was in all probability commissioned by Hedvig Eleonora; she plays an important role by drawing the eye to one of the central figures of the picture, the infant prince Karl, later Karl XII. Karl XI and Queen Ulrika Eleonora are at the ends of the group, which also includes the Princess Hedvig Sofia and De la Gardie's consort, Maria Euphrosyne, closely related to the royal family – in the folds of the drapery may be glimpsed a portrait of her brother, Karl X Gustav.

The reason for commissioning the portrait appears to have been that the *riksdag* of 1682–83 had strengthened and confirmed absolutism, that the succession had been extended to include female heirs, and that Prince Karl had been born. Ehrenstrahl himself comments that he wished to illustrate the happy state of the realm now that

*Allegory of the order of
succession. Painting by
D.K. Ehrenstrahl,
1693. National
Museum of Fine Arts.
Photo: The National
Swedish Art Museums.*

the royal throne had been secured. To a modern critic it is clear that for this purpose he has called on all his skill in composition and judicious use of colour and by combining his traditional group portrait with allegorical features. The two royal children are lifted out of their historical context by the idealization of their clothing. The prince is wearing the eternal blue and the imitation classicism of his sister's garments suggests the reddish light of dawn; in addition she acts as a classical goddess by crowning her brother with laurels, while he acknowledges the observer with a majestic gesture. The portrait has an apotheotic strain which further emphasizes the ceremonial and triumphal character of the painting.

Thus Ehrenstrahl was able to use the tool of his art to comment on the political course of events. In the *tableaux vivants* of the court festivities of the period there were similar groups, supplemented with allegorical images, and eulogistic literature takes on the same optimistic tone. But also when worldly triumph gave way to gloomy feelings of life's transience the court painter was at hand, as were poets and musicians, waiting to serve his masters. We see this in the paintings he produced in memory of the four princes who died in rapid succession in the 1680s. As well as perpetuating their memory, the pictures were to afford comfort by hinting at the life of the royal children in their eternal salvation. Ehrenstrahl handled the task by referring to the Catholic Baroque as then represented in Sweden by Nicodemus Tessin the Younger, the leading pageant master of the Caroline court. For the funerals in Riddarholm Church Tessin had designed magnificent sarcophagi which formed the centrepiece of *castra doloris*, an occasional architecture erected inside the church. To this funereal pomp were added obituaries composed by Lindschöld and dirges expressing the kingdom's collective dismay at the death of the princes in an array of symbols of mortality. The symbols recur in Ehrenstrahl's paintings and also in a number of cabinet pictures by the Dutchman Cornelis van Meulen, in his case juxtaposed with reproductions of the portrait busts of the princes sculpted by

Nicolaes Millich. The driving force behind all these orders was clearly the dowager queen, who could now extend her dynastic gallery at Drottningholm.

In the 1690s, Ehrenstrahl's tributes to the royal family culminate in a series of major allegories that conclude his work at Drottningholm. Here we find, amid a throng of figures, the settling of Swedo-Danish discord by the royal nuptials (1692), the peaceful rule of Karl XI (1695) and the exploits of the Swedish kings (1695). The most interesting is the allegory of the order of succession (1693). The painting shows Svecia passing on the regalia to the royal heirs, a cult ceremony performed in the presence of the four Estates of the realm, which together with other figures constitute a kind of participating assembly.

With its breadth of theme and the fixed grouping of the figures, the painting is a recapitulation of ideas already used by the painter on different occasions. The setting contains associations with both church and palace – perhaps the ceremony is taking place in the temple of Eternity. The personification of the virtues was of course intimately linked with the symbolism of the eternal, just as the immortality of fame was a constant theme of the literary panegyric. Once again, courtly drama provides the example pointing directly to Ehrenstrahl's picture: when the drama *Lykko-Prijs* (The Praise of Fortune) (1689) at last reaches its climax, it is Svecia who enters the temple of Eternity to wish the royal family good fortune and prosperity. With its sacral character and uncompromising loyalty to monarchic power the great allegory of the Estates forms the most striking conceivable contrast with the image once introduced by Schering Rosenhane back in the 1640s, when the Estates and the power of the sovereign were perfectly balanced. The state allegory at Drottningholm expresses absolutism as a political system.

When the Swedish people appear, in other words, they do so as personifications of the Estates. With their distinctive attributes they play their part on the political stage. The tall figure of the nobility is conspicuous with her helmet, armour and cloak strongly differentiating

Per Olsson, speaker of the Estate of the peasants at the riksdag. *Painting by D.K. Ehrenstrahl, 1686.* Photo: The National Swedish Art Museums.

her from the representative of the peasantry crouching over the support of her stick; her clothing is simple, she is rosy-cheeked and has ears of rye and cornflowers in her hair. On closer inspection the stick turns out to be a runic staff, the almanac of the Swedish farmer. The bending of the knees, showing deference to the other Estates, is dictated by the court painter's conception of the correct way to portray people from the lowest group in the social hierarchy. He had already shown his sensitivity to the social reference system governing the conduct of the figures on the historical stage. This may be further illustrated by another painting reminding us of the allegory of the Estates.

In 1686 Hedvig Eleonora instructed the court painter to paint a portrait of Per Olsson of Gladhammar, the speaker of the peasants' Estate at the *riksdag* of that year. The direct reason for this was that as the representative of his Estate the speaker had been one of the godfathers at the baptism of Prince Karl Gustav. As a gift to mark the occasion, the speaker received a silver jug and a hundred ducats, together with exemption of this own farm from taxation for the remainder of his life and his wife's. The commissioning of the portrait may also in part have been prompted by the important role of the commoner Estates at the *riksdagar* of 1680 and 1682 and the shift of political power towards absolutism. It is also in place to recall the strong position of the Swedish peasant in general, unique in Europe on account of the peasantry's ancient freedom from bondage.

The peasant is shown quite logically in a palatial setting which opens out behind him into an adjoining room where we glimpse a throne standing on a podium. Against this regal background the speaker appears in full figure, with his leather cap under his arm and leaning on a stick. His stance is hunched, his knees are bent; the painter has made telling use of the contrast between the strict horizontal-vertical effect of the room and the mobile contours of the black-clad figure. The peasant is depicted in the shadow of the throne but also as an individual with his own dignity – the knowing look gives character to the bearded face and he appeals to the sym-

pathies of the observer.

Another example of Ehrenstrahl's ability within the conventions of courtly art to give a convincing picture of a person far from the centres of power is to be seen in the portrait of the attendant at the spa of Medevi and his sons. Medevi was a spa discovered in 1677 by the physician Urban Hiärne; after having originally been owned by Councillor of the Realm Gustav Soop it was purchased by the dowager queen and quickly became a popular resort of courtiers and the aristocracy. Festivities were arranged at regular intervals and the court painter, too, found his way here in search of relief from the gout that was becoming worse as he grew older. It was the queen who gave him the task of portraying the spa attendant in the performance of his duties. The result calls to mind the Dutch genre pictures of the period, which were undoubtedly familiar to the artist, but the picture also has another dimension: the helpful faces are turned towards the same observers as looked at Per Olsson's portrait at Drottningholm; it is the power elite who are receiving the health-giving waters, just brought up from the spring.

How the aspirations of monarchic absolutism finally led to the building of Stockholm Palace and its adornment will not be dealt with in detail here. The ideas we encountered in the earlier periods of Caroline art are now developed on a large scale: to an even greater degree art now proclaims established facts, the array of virtues become manifestations of absolute monarchic power and the individual shades of meaning are increasingly replaced by conventional signs, while at the same time the higher ranks of the old nobility almost entirely lose the position they had as patrons of the arts and builders during the years of expansion before 1680.

Journeys of Exploration

The pictorial world we have so far been considering is deeply conditioned by the great-power dream. The use of potent symbols created a world in the imagination in which the new position of power acquired glamour and

The attendant at the spa and his sons of Medevi. Painting by D.K.
Ehrenstrahl, 1686. Gripsholm Palace.
Photo: The National Swedish Art Museums.

renown, whether the symbols were borrowed from humanism's arsenal of examples or from Gothic antiquity. But this is only one facet, albeit a very spectacular one, of seventeenth-century Sweden's visual culture. There were other areas in which illustration was required, areas in which the concern was not so much to support a position won as to explore new fields. Here, too, pictures were needed, but the nature of the tasks meant that they were of a very different form.

Ehrenstrahl was convinced in theory that art of value had to have a relationship with moral philosophy. The roots of this view lay in the Italian Renaissance, which had laid down the hierarchy of subjects – history, religion and classical mythology could offer more than enough, what lay hidden beneath them could not be made a subject of study at the increasingly influential academies. Nature and visible reality had to be made to conform to grand models, in particular the art of antiquity but also modern masters who could match reputations with their predecessors in Greece and Rome. The tacit assumption was a clientele which shared these ideals.

But pictures and the pictorial arts might also appeal to entirely different spheres of interest. When the Uppsala professor Johannes Schefferus, who came to Sweden during the reign of Queen Christina, published his book on painting, *Graphice, seu de arte pingendi*, in 1669, he made a point of reminding the reader of other subjects, such as brought into focus the realistic tradition in modern painting. Here illusion is more important than idealization; landscape, animals, the common people and scientific illustration made their distinct demands for visual acuity. Whereas the academic tradition was strong in Italy and France, in Holland it was totally overshadowed by the currents of realism. In Sweden, Ehrenstrahl's unique position at the Caroline court caused him to cultivate both strains, in apparent contradiction of his theoretical conviction, but very much in keeping with his role as a true servant of the king. His training put him in a position to satisfy requirements that lay far from the celebratory painting of royalty that he most

wished to practise. The reason for this was the particular nature of his clientele, especially in the burning interest of Karl XI in hunting, animals and nature; this came to be a rewarding challenge to the court painter. But other aspects of the physical world were also drawn into the artistic culture of the nation and required their documentation.

The enhancement of the external environment by an extensive programme of building demonstrated the country's capacity for creating impressive symbols of the new power status. The idea came readily to mind, therefore, of displaying the new architecture in the form of a patriotic illustrative project, in order to acquaint ill-informed foreigners with the magnificence of the cities and the remarkable ancient monuments of the country. Sweden's topography in all its diversity should be mapped out in pictorial form; so should the country's plant and animal kingdoms, in many respects exotic to a Continental readership. The Age of Greatness would in other words see a sequel to the description of the country's outstanding advantages that had once been supplied by Olaus Magnus when as an exile in the mid-sixteenth century he had written his history of the Nordic peoples. For him, too, illustration played an important part; but what in him was often the product of free imagination could now be subjected to a modern insistence on empiricism and precision.

The largest and most ambitious project was *Svecia antiqua et hodierna* (1716), to some extent inspired by German predecessors and with Quartermaster-General Erik Dahlbergh the leading spirit in its implementation. He was also to be responsible for the illustrations to Samuel Pufendorf's history of Karl X Gustav; furthermore, he produced drawings for Johan Philip Lembke's paintings at Drottningholm on the same monarch's martial feats. Dahlbergh had studied in Italy and was not only an artist but also a distinguished architect (he designed the memorial chapel of Field Marshal Lars Kagg which was mentioned earlier). In the course of extensive travels around the country he and his assistants made numerous drawings which were later transferred to copper by foreign engravers. It should at once be noted that the world that took shape in *Svecia antiqua* was not in every respect true to life; as in the art of panegyric oratory, the authors permitted themselves adjustments and additions that lent greater lustre to the whole undertaking. Assiduous though Dahlbergh was, the enormous work was never completed in its entirety; when the fortunes of war turned, early in the eighteenth century, the scope for such cultural shows of force was reduced. In place of the grandiloquent gestures came, with the advent of the Era of Liberty, an interest in the intimate, the utilitarian and the immediate, a different concept of the country's ability to assert itself internationally.

In the field of Gothic historical romanticism Dahlbergh's project had its counterpart in the *Atlantica* of Olof Rudbeck the Elder, a gigantic attempt to prove that Sweden was the cradle of all culture, a matrix of nations. The volume of plates begins with a frontispiece that may fairly be taken as indicative of its author's patriotic intentions. In the centre stands Rudbeck himself, in the guise of an anatomist dissecting the globe. He had in fact begun his career as a doctor and his greatest accomplishment was the discovery in the early 1650s of the lymphatic system, of which more below. Around him are grouped the sages of antiquity, filled with wonder at the remarkable things being revealed to their eyes: Plato and Aristotle rub shoulders with Ptolemy, Plutarch and Tacitus, all important contributors to Rudbeck's ingenious proofs. The point of the picture is that Rudbeck's historical research should be measured with the same demand for accuracy as his contributions to medical history. Even those who doubted would one day perceive the truth that was being manifested – beside Rudbeck stands, to be doubly sure, Father Time, pointing to Sweden, the island of the gods, the Atlantis written of by Plato and once lost beneath the sea. The background to this world stage is formed by the stars of the northern skies, the final seal on the transformation of scientific anatomy into patriotic archaeology. Not surprisingly, we find among the illustrations to the *Atlantica* analytical views of excavations, astonishingly

modern in method, which show different series of strata as a means of underpinning the chronological reasoning. (For a more detailed description of Rudbeck's archaeological method, see Gunnar Eriksson's contribution to this volume.)

But before Rudbeck became an archaeologist he had devoted himself to human anatomy. From the outset he shows himself aware of the potential pedagogic value of illustration. A pamphlet on the circulation of the blood (1652) is accompanied by a drawing, and in the copy in the university library at Uppsala there is also a water colour inspired by an earlier work on anatomy. When in the following year he published his work on the lymphatic system, his original drawings were engraved by an Uppsala student. It can truly be said here that the pictures help to chart previously unknown worlds. They not only reproduce what can be seen, they also make the new discoveries clearly visible.

Similar ambitions, but on an even grander scale, characterize Rudbeck's initiative in, as he put it, publishing a work which was to include "all the world's plants". The reproductions were to be life-sized. True to the patriotic ideology it was to be called *Campus Elysii*. With a large number of assistants Rudbeck began the work by painting water colours both from existing originals and from collected plants. The intention was then to transfer the pictures to wooden blocks for printing and colouring. Unfortunately, the finished blocks fell victim to the flames in the devastating Uppsala fire of 1702. No more than one volume of the planned work had been published.

The interest in botany and natural history was shared by Rudbeck's son, Olof Rudbeck the Younger. His work *Propagatio plantarum* (1680) is now regarded as marking the introduction of modern botany in Sweden. The illustrations with which he provided the book give a hint of what was to come in the 1690s, when he was engaged in another of the patriotic illustrational projects – one dealing with the natural history of Lapland.

Interest in the culture of the Saami (Lapps) had been considerably stimulated by Johannes Schefferus' book

Lapponia (1674), a broad survey of conditions in Sweden's most northerly province, which also contained a few illustrations. In 1694 Karl XI travelled to the Finnish border to see the midnight sun. His experiences came to have some bearing on the expedition that was fitted out the following year, with astronomers in the company and Rudbeck the Younger as the expert on flora and fauna; the expedition also included artists, and a couple of young nobleman who made use of the opportunity of an educational trip with rather a difference. For Rudbeck's part, the intention was to gather material for a work concerned chiefly with Nordic ornithology; that the journey was motivated by genuine curiosity is apparent from the sketch book that has been preserved. It reports from a number of different fields. Some of the pictures are by Rudbeck but others are by his assistant, Andreas Holtzbom; both were skilful draughtsmen and water colourists. As in the case of *Svecia*, there were foreign predecessors who had made similar journeys of exploration; here the pages are filled with reproductions, some of which have been lightly sketched while others have been executed with the greatest precision of detail. They convey a vivid impression of the landscape that met the travellers, owing nothing to studies in earlier literature. The collection opens with Holtzbom's magnificent panorama of the falls at Kaskawari, a bird's eye view of the Lapland wilderness with a solitary Saami tent as the only sign of man's existence. The sketch book also contains extremely naturalistic illustrations of mountain fish that have been pulled out of the streams, botanical specimens of various kinds, and lichens, which are a miracle of sharp-sighted reproduction. In some cases the sketches were used for the remarkable illustrations in Rudbeck's book of birds, prepared between 1695 and 1708 and intended to be printed with hand-coloured copper engravings. Rudbeck's proud concept, at least on a par with his father's botanical project, was never realized, even though more than 200 water colours were produced and, indeed, used by Rudbeck in his lectures in zoology in the 1720s. But what he did achieve is sufficient to give him a place of

esteem in the history of ornithological illustration.

When Conrad Gesner and Giuseppe Aldrovandi laid the foundations of modern zoology in the sixteenth century they were well aware of the value of illustration. Like Linnaeus many years later, they were convinced that a picture could reveal things that the most detailed verbal description could not. But the woodcuts in their weighty tomes were for the most part coarse and not very accurate; visual formulas were propagated which later obscured rather than clarified the specific appearance of the creatures concerned. There was the additional problem of lack of colour – the plant and animal illustrations in the illuminated manuscripts of the late Middle Ages displayed a higher standard of accuracy in representation, but development was temporarily interrupted when the mass-produced illustration made its appearance.

Rudbeck's overriding principle was that the birds must be depicted life-sized, reproducing the colouring of the plumage as seen in live birds. It is a known fact that the colours quickly fade after the bird has been shot; to the keenly observant Rudbeck it seemed essential to have access to fresh specimens and he therefore obtained royal permission to spend what was necessary on the project. What is new and remarkable is the patient work that has gone into the details, from the general tonal character to the specific delineation of the feathers. So the birds parade past, from eagle, crane and capercaillie down to the smallest member of the Swedish fauna, the goldcrest. When Linnaeus saw the pictures he was delighted – it was incredible that they could be the work of a human hand! As illustrated works of ornithology began to appear in England and Germany in the first half of the eighteenth century – from authors such as Frisch, Albin and Edwards – it was not realized that the true pioneer was in fact a professor at Uppsala, on the very margins of Europe. Only recently has Rudbeck's book been published in a facsimile edition, together with a modern commentary.

Interest in natural history and the descriptive picture stemmed from the empirical research tradition initiated by Francis Bacon at the start of the seventeenth century. All over Europe we find a pictorial practice that has developed more or less independently of the enormous authority of the humanist tradition. We have already seen how in Caroline Sweden Ehrenstrahl implemented his conviction that the task of art was the glorification of the sovereign by also allowing room for pictures of a realistic flavour. As has been mentioned, the king was an enthusiastic hunter, who enjoyed nothing better than to sally forth into the countryside of central Sweden in pursuit of game. What he experienced on such expeditions is reported by Ehrenstrahl in a style that might be called congenial – we quickly appreciate that this king would have been concerned to support Rudbeck's natural history project. It may therefore be of interest to follow the king and his court painter out into the country – we happen to know that Ehrenstrahl sometimes stayed at one of the places frequented by the king and his shooting companions.

In 1674 he painted his famous study of the blackcocks' lek, now in the National Museum. It is an early morning in April. The sun is about to rise over the glimmering rosy landscape that opens between coulisses of firs and birch stems. In the foreground the blackcocks are displaying, while the royal shooting party can be dimly seen in a hide close by. The picture is both a landscape and a hunting scene, and bears witness to a meticulous study of the birds and their movements. The painter has clearly examined and copied shot birds with great care, well aware that the result will be subjected to expert scrutiny. The principles of the Italian Baroque may be sensed behind the composition and the lighting, but the painting is nevertheless unique in its European context. If the strict formality of the gardens of the palaces and stately homes conveys a tribute to the owner, what we have here is a tribute to the sovereign which lies outside the norms and conventions – the contrast with what is reported in, for example, scenes from the hunts of the Spanish court is very evident. Using his own experience and knowledge, the Swedish court painter has made his own journey of discovery in worlds to which Rudbeck

Kestrel.
From O. Rudbeck the Younger's Book of Birds.
Photo: Olle Lindman

and his followers gave a decidedly scientific treatment.

In some cases Ehrenstrahl himself approaches a scientific intention in his pictures, as when he depicts a pair of blackcocks hanging against a boarded partition, an example of the style of painting known as *trompe l'oeil*, where the aim is to create an illusion that deceives the viewer. Furthest of all from *Dygdens odödliga belöning* is the still life of a magnificent melon, painted in 1678 and furnished with an inscription stating its weight and where it was cultivated. The two paintings indicate the range of an unusually versatile artistry.

Mentality and Visual Competence

The history of art is indisputably a history of styles. Even if we no longer presuppose cyclical processes, it is clear that styles burgeon, bloom and fade. Seen from this perspective, the history of Swedish art during the Great Powder-period may seem to take a relatively uncomplicated course, from the late Manneristic phase with its residual sixteenth-century ideals to the breakthrough of the Baroque tendencies that were to set their stamp on developments from the middle of the century and which also left their mark in other sectors of aesthetic culture. But the works of art and their stylistic features did not operate in a vacuum, they were a response to specific needs, articulated with varying degrees of clarity, which immediately bring into play the role of the public and the patron. The external circumstances and the frequency of the allegorical ideas that also sought expression in the pictures influenced and complicated the mechanics of the course of events.

The Swedish situation was long dominated by the company of painters in Stockholm, a part of the guild organization and always ready to defend its privileges against artists whose employment at the court or by the aristocracy exempted them from their obligations to the guild. There were corresponding organizations in France (*La Maîtrise*) and elsewhere on the Continent (the Brotherhoods of St. Luke). Such an organization was not conductive to any revolutionary changes of style.

With Queen Christina comes the definitive change in the artistic and cultural climate of Sweden. Imported painters, such as David Beck, Sébastien Bourdon and Abraham Wuchters, helped to give artistic life a dynamic pulse that had been missing in the retarded climate of the preceding era, and Ehrenstrahl successfully completed the transition. New customs and channels of communication, including a more intensive contact with foreign countries, created a healthy social competition, and with it a more favourable reception for the new fashions, artistic and intellectual, which now made their breakthrough. In addition, the visual arts came also to help the country by presenting the face to the outside world, and in particular to France, that befitted a great power. The artistic efforts and, indeed, the use of imagery and of visual documentation in general came to function within the overall system of symbols that has earlier been somewhat tentatively referred to as the patriotic ideology. Despite the various slight differences, there is a common theme linking the grandiose imagery on the royal ship "Wasa", the ensemble of architecture, sculpture and inscriptions of the Palace of the Nobility, and Ehrenstrahl's political allegories at Drottningholm. It may be detected behind the patriotic illustrative projects, whether they dealt with topography and impressive buildings or the natural history of the Swedish *fjäll*. Pictures made it possible to express the dream of an internal splendour that could live up what had been attained by military triumph on the battlefields of Europe. A visual competence developed to meet the varying needs of the great power.

Perhaps the patriotic ideology reflects the particular mentality of the groups who competed to take the crucial decisions and thus guided the march of events. The visual culture of the bourgeoisie was insignificant – the distinctive initiatives were taken by the monarchy and the aristocracy, and supported by the world of learning. When the political circumstances changed, the visual culture changed with them, as quickly and dramatically as once it had taken shape at the dawn of the Age of Greatness.

References

Dahlgren, S., Ellenius, A., Gustafsson, L. & Larsson, G., *Kultur och samhälle i stormaktstidens Sverige* (1967).

Ellenius, A., "David Klöcker Ehrenstrahl" in *David Klöcker Ehrenstrahl* (National Swedish Museum of Fine Arts, 1976).

– *De arte pingendi. Latin Art Literature in Seventeenth-Century Sweden and its International Background*, Lychnos-Bibliotek 19 (1960).

– *Den atlantiska anatomin. Ur bildkonstens idéhistoria* (1984).

– "Die repräsentative Funktion der adligen Bauten und ihrer Ausstattung im schwedischen 17. Jahrhundert" in *Arte et Marte. Studien zur Adelskultur des Barockzeitalters in Schweden, Dänemark und Schleswig-Holstein,* ed. D. Lohmeier (1978).

– "Olof Rudbeck d.y. och den naturalhistoriska bildtradition" in *Fogelboken av Olof Rudbeck d.y.* (1985, Eng. trans. *Olof Rudbeck's Book of Birds,* Stockholm 1986).

– "Gustav Adolf i bildkonsten: från *Miles Christianus* till nationell frihetssymbol" in *Gustav II Adolf – 350 år efter Lützen* (1982).

– "Imago Iustitiae. Till Rättvisans ikonografi under stormaktstiden" in *Rättshistoriska studier,* Series II, Vol. IX (1984).

– *Karolinska bildidéer,* Ars Suetica 1 (1966).

– "Symbol och verklighet" in *Magnus Gabriel De la Gardie* National Swedish Museum of Fine Arts exhibition catalogue no. 434 (1980).

Gustafsson, L., *Virtus Politica. Politisk etik och nationellt svärmeri i den tidigare stormaktstidens litteratur,* Lychnos-Bibliotek 15 (1956).

Johannesson, K., *I polstjärnans tecken. Studier i svensk barock,* Lychnos-Bibliotek 24 (1968).

Magnusson, B., *Att illustrera fäderneslandet – en studie i Erik Dahlberghs verksamhet som tecknare,* Ars Suetica 10 (1986).

Soop, H., *The Power and the Glory. The Sculptures of the Warship Wasa* (1986).

Steneberg, K.E., *Kristinatidens måleri* (1955).

Uppsala University. The Gustavianum, built c. 1620.
Photo: Olle Lindman

Science and Learning in the Baroque Era

GUNNAR ERIKSSON

Even after Sweden became a great power in the early seventeenth century, it remained, as far as intellectual stimulus is concerned, almost entirely a recipient and scarcely a giver at all. There are several reasons for this. The break in religious continuity is one important factor. This break had occurred when Sweden went over from Catholicism to Protestantism under Gustav Vasa. With this, the highest intellectual life of the country largely collapsed. Sweden's only university from Catholic times, that in Uppsala, was virtually inactive after 1520. The monasteries were emptied and their treasuries of books and manuscripts scattered, not least because the parchment could be used in government offices to bind the accounts of the bailiffs. The first Protestant kings were little concerned with the cultivation of learning, despite the fact that they were well aware of the lack of well-trained native civil servants. By comparison with the sixteenth century, the seventeenth brought an intellectual springtime, but spring came only after the bleakest of winters.

The Role of the University

Another important factor behind the passive and purely receptive impression was the structure of the country's academic life. At the start of the century Europe was seeing the intellectual revolution constituted by the advance of modern science. It is a well-known fact that the seats of this modern science were not in the universities, which were traditionally closely allied with the Church, but in special newly established academies or in more or less tightly knit circles representing secularized interests in commerce, technology and politics. Such circles hardly existed in Sweden, and there were certainly no well-organized academies; what could be offered in the way of scholarship was concentrated in universities, and for the first third of the century there existed only the one in Uppsala. This had been reopened in 1593, and in the 1620s it was allocated the material resources to ensure teaching of a good quality.

But the ideology and instruction at Swedish universities did not greatly differ from those at most Continental seats of learning. The emphasis here, as there, was on religion, a religion which, rather than favour the rise of new scientific ideas, generally tended to obstruct them. The Function of the University of Uppsala was long decreed by ecclesiastical interests. These were unequivocal: it was of paramount importance to safeguard the Lutheran faith and therefore to train clergy who were firm in this faith. This had vital implications for teaching in philosophy, natural science and medicine. For, paradoxically enough, Lutheran theology was based just as firmly as the Catholic faith on the Aristotelian scholasticism that was the traditional substance of learning, and both, therefore, had an interest in opposing the new enemy of Aristotelianism: modern science and its radical picture of the world. It was the doctrinal controversy between the churches that had brought about this state of affairs. The Thirty Years' War, which had such a critical influence on the political destiny of Sweden, was also a spiritual war, fought with spiritual weapons. And in that struggle it was essential to be at least as well armed as the adversary. Scholasticism and logic provided these weapons, which had been ground extra

69

sharp by the renaissance of Aristotelian studies which had taken place in the sixteenth century and whose results were used first by the Catholic Counter-Reformation and quickly enough afterwards by its opponents.

Modern science, with the Copernican system as its foremost symbol, thus had no natural institutional or material base at the start of the seventeenth century. On the contrary, there was much in the Swedish setting that was inimical to the new ideas, as they flew in the face of current philosophy and rested on a very insecure tradition. That these ideas could eventually become accepted here in Sweden was probably due to the fact that the interests of those in power were not, after all, entirely homogeneous – there were cracks in the ideological wall. It is true that the Swedish state, in the shape of the powerful sovereign and his leading ministers, was highly concerned to maintain Lutheran orthodoxy, for the Protestant Church of Sweden was an established church with the king at its head. Keeping the population docile with the aid of a strong faith was a part of the exercise of political power. But at the same time the territorial expansion that followed the successful wars greatly increased the need for well-trained temporal administrators. The only places that could lay the foundation of a sound training for administration were the universities, first and foremost, as already mentioned, the one in Uppsala and later the new universities founded during the century at Åbo (Finland), Dorpat (in the Baltic provinces), Greifswald (on captured German soil) and Lund (in the recently regained Skåne). Even though a useful system of training civil servants was instituted within the government offices themselves, where novices observed the workings of their department for a period as ”auscultants”, this expansion of the universities was indispensable. For that reason the highest authorities had an interest in seeing that the universities were not preoccupied to the exclusion of all else with the training of the clergy and thus with the subjects and attitudes that were required for the preaching of the Church. In their opinion room had also to be given to practical temporal subjects such as rhetoric, languages and science – a command of which would be of use to the prospective administrator or politician; indeed, such worldly studies were encouraged from the highest quarter, although initially with only partial success.

Thanks to this secularized interest, new ideas and a more modern spirit were able gradually to penetrate the universities. And by the end of the century they had, despite all the obstacles, become irresistible – scholasticism was buried, and the way to a new scientific epoch was open even in this northern corner of the world.

New Currents

Whereas traditional philosophy had its prophet in Aristotle, the opposing currents of ideas had prophets of their own. The two who undoubtedly had most influence on thinking in Sweden were both Frenchmen – Petrus Ramus and René Descartes. The ideas of Ramus made their mark at Uppsala University by the second decade of the seventeenth century, or perhaps earlier, having arrived principally via the universities of North Germany, which were much frequented by Swedish students. This educational reformer, still hardly touched by the new spirit of science, urged that instruction must be more practical, with the emphasis on politically and economically useful subjects such as rhetoric and natural philosophy, and that scholastic logic and its sophistries, often expressed in dog Latin, should be replaced by a clear, simple, ”Socratic” logic, framed in impeccable classical Latin and deliberately designed to serve the needs of practical living rather than the theological studies that had been the highest purpose of scholasticism. Seen from the standpoint of modern science, Ramism was hardly radical – moreover it had been formulated much too early in the intellectual development of Europe (Ramus died in 1572) and its originator was too enamoured of the great models of antiquity to wish to break with the principles of the traditional cosmology. But the programme was suffi-

René Descartes (Cartesius). Portrait by David Beck. Photo: Augusto Mendes

ciently temporal in its orientation to gain the goodwill of the Swedish authorities. It is likely that Ramism would have had a longer-lasting impact on Swedish university teaching than it did, had not another philosophy won the minds of many of the pious professors. For almost contemporaneously with Ramism arose the movement usually known as neo-Aristotelianism, encouraged by the growing polemic between the warring churches as the Counter-Reformation gained strength. This neo-Aristotelianism – like Ramism – had in fact a good deal in common with traditional scholasticism, but its armoury of concepts included all that could be added to the philosophical tradition by a renewed study of Aristotle's own writings in the original Greek texts, i.e. a study which bypassed the unsatisfactory medieval translations of the philosopher's works. As this neo-Aristotelianism suited the religious zealots of the universities – who were far from scarce – better than the worldly Ramism, and as the Church was very strong in Sweden, neo-Aristotelianism soon became the dominant philosophy. Not until the 1660s did the modernists return to the attack against the established truths, this time with the backing of a more telling authority, the sagacious universalist René Descartes.

The First Cartesian Controversy

Intellectually and in terms of resources, Uppsala remained the leading university throughout the seventeenth century. We may therefore confine our attentions to Uppsala, while bearing in mind that the pattern of events there can also be seen with varying degrees of clarity at the other Swedish universities.

At Uppsala the revolt against the prevailing scholasticism began in the small medical faculty, which consisted of only two professors – but two lions: Petrus Hoffwenius (1630–1682) and Olaus Rudbeck (1630–1702). The former was the most ardent Cartesian and the leading polemicist, the latter the most creative and original scientist in seventeenth-century Sweden. Both had received parts of their medical training in Holland, where the universities were strongly influenced by Cartesianism, and the University of Leiden, in particular, had begun to gain a reputation as one of the outstanding seats of learning in Europe. While there, they had ample opportunity to hear Cartesian doctrines expounded, and it was natural for this to be reflected in their teaching at Uppsala. Hoffwenius, in particular, presented the new ideas consistently and repeatedly, both in his lectures and in the disputations characteristic of the period, in which students had to defend a thesis as an exercise or in order to obtain their degree – a thesis that was often written by the professor and always defended under his supervision. Rumours of the new direction being taken by the teaching of medicine spread quickly in the little university city and protests were soon pouring in from representatives of the faculties of arts and sciences and of theology, where Aristotelianism was still well entrenched. A series of disputes arose, fought out in written form in, for example, dissertations for and against the new ideas or orally at meetings of the various administrative bodies of the university, where on one or two occasions the king's special representative, the university chancellor, intervened to try settle the dissension. The arguments advanced by the respective parties soon became those well known from the Continent and assumed a stereotyped form. It was more often the traditional scholasticists who took the offensive and the modernists who found themselves on the defensive. The chief objection raised by traditionalists and churchmen to the modernists was one which had already met Galileo at his inquisition. It concerned Copernicus' assertion that it was the sun that was stationary at the centre of the universe and not, as Aristotle and Ptolemy taught, the earth. The Copernican theory had been accepted – with certain equivocations – by Descartes, who generally embraced the ideas of modern science and gave them a firm philosophical substructure. The objection to Cartesianism was that the teaching of Copernicus was contrary to the word of the Bible, to God's own pronouncements in the Holy Scriptures, which had been dictated letter by letter by the Almighty. For according to the Book of Joshua God had commanded the sun to stand still in Gibeon – an incongruous order if the sun was already stationary. The Swedish Cartesians answered as Galileo and their Dutch predecessors had once answered, that God had had to express himself in a way that the people of the time of the Old Testament would understand, and at a date so far back in time everyone had of course imagined that the sun normally moved and the earth stood still. But to this the orthodox then retorted that the modernists were accusing God of lying – an unprecedented blasphemy. This was often the crucial point in the Church's condemnation of the new ideas, but of course the ideas also implied a radical transformation of the way of thinking on worldly matters, so radical that it would have been difficult to accept even without the question of the Biblical interpretation. The philosophy formulated by Aristotle, which the scholasticists had inherited and the Church had adopted, showed a meaningful world that moved and lived on the basis of an inner striving towards the realization of the essential in every object. It was a world which was ultimately guided by final causes. In the universe of the modernists, the laws of blind mechanics prevailed. This had been underlined by none other than their great prophet, Descartes. The soul which, according to Aristotle, resided in every living creature, including animals, plants and the heavens that governed the motion of the earth, was strictly distinguished from the corporeal. But to Descartes all space was corporeal, and the particles of which it was composed did not affect each other except by mechanical pressure. Only in man was there a peculiar connection between body and soul; in other respects the world as we see it was based on mechanics – this applied not only to the courses of the stars and to a stone falling to earth but also to the growth and ripening of plants, the flight of birds and the behaviour of animals. To the Aristotelians all this appeared absurd, and in dissertation after dissertation they dismissed such grotesque fancies, whereas the modernists heaped scorn on the guardians of religion for their insistence on crediting both animals and plants with an immortal soul.

These, therefore, were the questions at the centre of the row that blew up in the 1660s, when Petrus Hoffwenius started to lecture on natural philosophy according to the doctrines of Cartesianism. A demand for censorship of medical themes was raised, mainly from the Estate of the clergy in the *riksdag,* whereas the university's own theologians, although obviously opposed to the new trend, were notably more circumspect in calling for intervention by higher authorities. Within the university it was widely hoped to be able to treat the dispute as an internal matter. If Church and state leaders became too alarmed, there was a decided risk that the traditional privileges of the universities would be questioned and curtailed – and no professor really wanted that. But feelings ran high, and the quarrel was not to be confined to a purely theoretical and intellectual plane for long. Clashes of personality soon came to play a major part, and everyone guarded his own interests jealously. The two professors of medicine became so indignant at the accusations and the threat of censorship that they in turn threatened to suspend all teaching. When the discord became too great to ignore, the chancellor of the university, Magnus Gabriel De la Gardie, quite clearly made an attempt to pour oil on troubled waters. Eventually Hoffwenius agreed to keep Descartes out of his teaching, and the quarrel degenerated into an increasingly petty bickering about details which, on the surface at least, appeared a long way removed from the matters of principle that had formed the frontline.

Science and Medicine in the Second Half of the Seventeenth Century

Thus the 1670s became an interlude in the history of the Cartesian struggles at Uppsala, during which open strife about philosophical matters was unusual but important ideological changes were taking place behind the scenes. We can make use of this pause to take a closer look at the terms on which natural sciences were studied at the university. It was without doubt in this group of subjects that there was the greatest potential for a successful modernist breakthrough. As we have seen, the stronghold of the modern ideas was the small medical faculty, with its two professors. One was professor of theoretical medicine, the other of practical medicine. But there was really no clearly defined boundary between their two disciplines, and each took an almost global view of his subject field. Medicine obviously included such sciences as human anatomy and pharmacology, but these subjects required prior studies ranging over different branches of natural history, including botany, zoology and mineralogy. Such studies were therefore under the purview of the faculty of medicine, as, indeed, were large areas of physics and chemistry, since these apparently far-removed disciplines contained principles of relevance to an understanding of the more visibly related sciences. In this way the two chairs in medicine formed the centre of gravity of the whole scientific curriculum of the university. In the faculty of arts and sciences the natural sciences were represented by the three professorships in mathematics, of which one was given the name the "Euclidean" and specialized in geometry and arithmetic, one was the "Archimedean" with its emphasis on pure physics, and one was called the "Ptolemaic", its chief concern being astronomy. When the structure of traditional scholastic philosophy, with its consistent demand for universality, is recalled, it is hardly noteworthy that even the professor of theoretical philosophy could deal with scientific matters in his teaching.

That the three chairs in mathematics had been set up in the faculty is explicable in the light of what was said initially about the authorities' interest in partially secularizing the university and thereby creating a recruiting ground for temporal offices as well as the Church. This was an excellent opportunity for Cartesianism to make inroads into the faculty of arts and sciences. Just as Descartes himself had stressed the utility of sciences that could revolutionize medicine and technology, so his devotees could well point out that modem science was far more widely and successfully applicable in practical contexts than the traditional Aristotelian study of nature. If the traditionalists at the university were inclined to invoke the authority of the Bible as their main objection to the new physics, the best argument of the modernists against scholasticism was the potential usefulness of this new physics in the fortifications administration, the artillery and other technical spheres. In this respect it was often conceded on the orthodox side that the modernists were better equipped. This indicated that the argument was a very persuasive one and undoubtedly had the ear of the authorities. When the chancellor of the university listened to the cases put by both parties, he clearly wished to mediate. And that the state with all its power took a conciliatory rather than a directly rejectionist position was itself a half-victory for the modernists.

In actual fact there was some movement in the modernists' position during the relatively tranquil 1670s. This occurred in several ways. For one thing, there was a continuous influx of Cartesian ideas, via many different channels, and for another at least one representative of the modem camp, Rudbeck, achieved things that seemed to confirm the vigour and practicality of the new ideas. Hoffwenius, who had been made to promise to give up his Cartesian lectures, quietly resumed them after a few years. His teaching must also have been important to many students in the faculty of arts and sciences, who were far more numerous than the very small band who ventured to study medicine in the backwater of Sweden. At the same time, many students continued to go abroad for periods of varying length, mainly to Germany and Holland, where Cartesianism was steadily consolidating its status. They came home confirmed in the new way of thinking, or maybe converted to it. An example of how the new philosophy had infiltrated the ranks of the senior students is provided by Nicolaus Celsius (1658–1724); who in 1679 presented the dissertation *De principiis astronomicis propriis,* in which the Copernican theory was openly presented as accepted fact. But this was not allowed to pass unchallenged. The theologians reacted by demanding the power to censor the dissertation. Celsius composed a written defence that, in the eyes of the theologians, only made matters worse. This was because he used the classical Galilean argument that God, in commanding the sun to stand still, had been choosing his words to suit the comprehension of the common man – a claim that the theologians had angrily rejected long ago. Celsius' disputation never took place, and to that extent the Aristotelians retained a grip on the situation, but it was an increasingly precarious one.

In the meantime the other professor of medicine, Olaus Rudbeck, was also working for the cause of modernism, albeit in his own very individual way – one which could not lead directly to the goal. Rudbeck was never a true Cartesian, but he was anti-scholastic and a warm supporter of the principles of the new science, of empiricism and experimentation. He was the first Swede to make an original scientific discovery of any significance. While still a young student of twenty, he carried out a long series of anatomical examinations of dogs, cats and other mammals, resulting in his discovery of the lymphatic vessels and their system, hitherto largely unknown to science. (Cf. Allan Ellenius above). He demonstrated his findings to Queen Christina in 1652 and published them with his own illustrations in 1653, the year in which the Danish physician Bartholin announced the same discovery. It is quite clear that the two Scandinavian scientists had been totally unaware of each other's work, but a heated dispute over priority flared up in the customary manner.

Rudbeck's discovery of the lymphatic system is relevant to the cause of modernism in Sweden, as the manner of his presenting it shows that even in the 1650s he was already a believer in modern mechanistic principles. This is particularly shown by his acceptance of the new theory of the movements of the blood in the human body that was put forward by William Harvey in 1628. Harvey had of course discovered the circulation of the blood and described the heart as a pump, a comparison that his successors interpreted in a mechanistic spirit. Descartes accepted Harvey's view with enthusiasm and saw in the Englishman's discovery one of the best proofs that mechanistic interpretation of the living organism was the correct one. Rudbeck was able to show that the lymphatic vessels that were connected to the liver carried a milky fluid, chyle, away from this organ. According to the traditionalists, this fluid should instead be carried to the liver and converted there into blood. Rudbeck's discoveries were consistent with the new theory of circulation.

In another early publication, the Uppsala dissertation *De circulatione sanguinis,* Rudbeck explicitly defended the modern view of the course taken by the blood in the bodies of humans and animals. The renown earned by Rudbeck for his anatomical researches naturally enhanced the prestige of modern science, and of its ally Cartesianism, in Sweden. In the 1660s the multitalented Rudbeck, now professor of medicine, studied the path of a comet and published a detailed and informative letter on it in a Continental standard work on comets. Here he was able, in passing, to admit his Copernican convictions and, just like Descartes, to reject all superstitious notions of comets as ill omens, consigning them instead to the category of natural bodies in the solar system, governed by the laws of mechanics. This letter also contained a contribution to the feud at the University of Uppsala, in which he announced that he had burned a number of manuscripts on natural philosophy in his bitterness at the illwill he had encountered among his conservative colleagues at the university.

Rudbeck also made an impressive scientific contribution as a botanist. He began on the gigantic project of illustrating all the world's plants, using the most comprehensive catalogue available, Caspar Bauhin's *Pinax theatri botanici.* Rudbeck gave his work the title *Campus Elysii,* and had some 6,000 woodcuts ready for it by 1702, when a devastating fire in Uppsala reduced virtually the whole project to ashes. (Cf. Allan Ellenius). He also – and perhaps this was of more importance – laid out a botanical garden in Uppsala, the first in the history of the university. Here, every spring and autumn, he instructed students in plant science, a distinct advance for empirical botany and thus in accordance with one of the

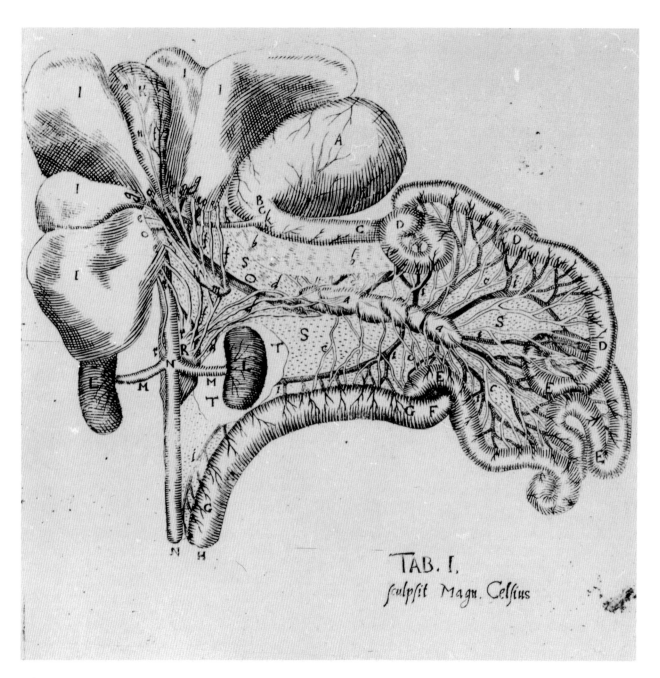

TAB. I.

fculpfit Magn. Celfius

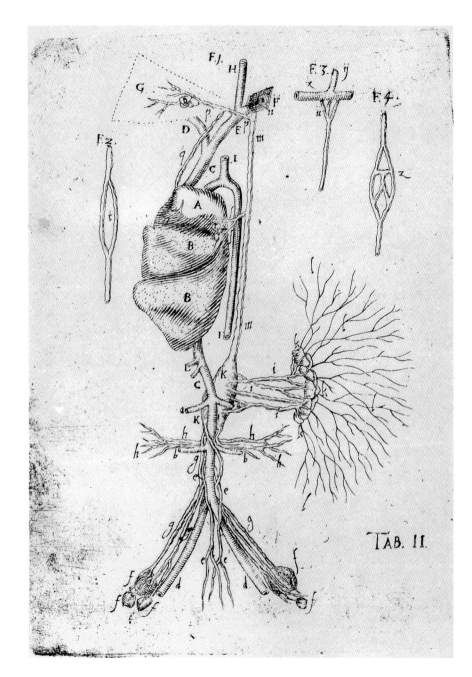

The lymphatic vessels and their systems. Olof Rudbeck the Elder's own illustration. Uppsla University Library. Photo: Uppsala University Library.

cherished principles of modern science – that one should read from the book of nature rather than rely on the writings of previous authorities. Both *Campus Elysii* and the botanical garden foretokened the epoch-making contribution to natural history so closely linked with the name of Linnæus in the following century, which was to bring so much success for Swedish science. In this chain of development Rudbeck's son, Olof Rudbeck the Younger, was an important link. But the advent of the garden also had social consequences: it brought Rudbeck fame as a landscape gardener and he was soon employed by the higher nobility, and in particular by no less a person than Magnus Gabriel De la Gardie, the chancellor of the university. That this gave him greater prestige and thus indirectly advanced the cause of modernism is beyond doubt.

Rudbeck had outstanding technical ability in general, which he used on innumerable occasions in and outside the university. It is of interest to note, for example, that he gave instruction in technical subjects and that in connection with this he set up three small-scale manufactories along the river that flows through Uppsala. He was also responsible for a lot of building work, such as the erection of a large establishment for the exercises of the students of the nobility in fencing, riding, dancing, drawing and moden languages, and a truly magnificent anatomical theatre in the main building of the university. All this underlined his importance to the university and also, indirectly, the fact that the new science that he represented was of great importance in practical contexts. Even if the link between these practical projects and the theories of modern science may appear rather weak to us today, it was obvious that his contemporaries saw and believed in such a connection.

The Second Cartesian Controversy

During the 1680s it became ever more clear that all the faculties except theology (i.e. arts and sciences, medicine and law) had accepted Cartesianism or, at least, abandoned Aristotelianism. The process of moderniz-ation had unobtrusively transformed the whole picture of the world that was to be inculcated by the university. But the old school did not give in without one final effort. The combination of new professors in the faculty of theology and a belligerent Estate of the clergy in the *riksdag* led to a sudden counterattack in the autumn of 1686. Inspired by the professor of theology, Schütz – a man who hated Rudbeck, the Estate of the clergy sent a petition to the king, Karl XI, asking for the faculty of theology to be authorized to prohibit undesirable disputations in other faculties. The reason given for this request was that Cartesianism, which was dangerous to the Church and the faith, had begun to spread alarmingly. The result of this petition was that the king, following a bureaucratic routine familiar in Sweden even in those early days, circulated the petition to the four faculties of the university for their opinions. The replies were formulated and returned in the spring of 1687. This exchange is what is known in the history of Swedish science as "the second Cartesian controversy".

The reply of the faculties was what one might have expected. In various tones the three secular faculties deplored any suggestion of outside censorship and pointed out the superiority of the new philosophy and its importance to society. Only the theologians, as was equally to be expected, endorsed the Estate of the clergy's recommendation. The king's decision came in the autumn. Its content has been debated. The king declared that study should be free – and this has been interpreted as the final defeat of scholasticism. But the sentence declaring freedom carried a proviso: "so long as this is not contrary to the word of God." And that has led others to see it as a decision by Karl XI in favour of the theologians and the clergy. For, as we have noted, it was the fact that Copernicanism was indeed contrary to the word of God in the Book of Joshua that was one of the main points of the orthodox attack on modernism. What, then *did* it mean? What the king really wanted to say, of course, we can never find out. But we can see what did in fact happen at the university – this educational institution that was now entirely in the power of the monarch. No censorship of the kind advocated by the theologians was ever introduced. When Johan Bilberg, a Cartesian and leading natural scientist, was moved from the professorship he had surprisingly obtained in the faculty of theology, he moved diagonally upwards, becoming vicar of an important Swedish town, Örebro, and very soon the bishop of Strängnäs, which gave him the supervision of one of Sweden's oldest and most influential *gymnasia*. A young Cartesian, Erik Castovius, had his academic career interrupted after publishing two controversial dissertations in the 1690s. But what was objectionable in these was not that he revealed Cartesian sympathies but that he questioned monarchic absolutism. And a few years into the next century the theologians themselves were Cartesians or, at least, they had all abandoned Aristotle and scholasticism.

Classical Studies and Philology

The Cartesian controversies at Uppsala University are without doubt the most important events in the intellectual history of Sweden in the seventeenth century. They marked the fact that the country's intellectual life had attained a certain breadth and wealth of variety and was now forging links with modern Europe. Sweden could take an honourable place in the circle of learned nations. But the biggest impact was on science, whereas the humanities, which were studied by far larger numbers of students, were affected by these feuds only very indirectly. Nonetheless, the humanities may also be said to have made important advances during the seventeenth century – in the quantity and range of teaching offered, in particular, but also in its quality. Nor were the humanities spared from enlivening controversy, although here this can be touched on only briefly.

The firm and, for a long time, unshaken foundation of humanist learning was the study of classical languages, and the philology associated with it, which in the seventeenth century included the study not only of Latin and Greek from a purely linguistic aspect but also of the

whole culture expressed in these languages. Classical languages formed the main content of the education given in lower schools and occupied a dominant position in the range of subjects at the universities, where Latin, Greek, poetry and oratory each had at least one professor. Philology reached the Continental level in the 1620s, when Uppsala began to recruit men of outstanding talent from Europe to fill what was known as the Skyttean chair in politics and rhetoric. The most eminent of these was Johannes Schefferus (1621–1679, educated at Strasbourg and Leiden and professor at Uppsala from 1647), who quickly settled in Swedish surroundings without losing touch with his contacts abroad.

Medal depicting Johannes Schefferus, by Arvid Karlsteen. Royal Coin Cabinet.
Photo: ATA.

Schefferus became celebrated for his studies of Roman chariots and other vehicles and for similar work in the field of cultural philology, and also for his scholarly description of Sweden's northernmost province, Lapland, and other research in Swedish history. In his work he stood for a sober modern objectivity, which to some extent contrasts with the patriotic excesses that characterized a number of purely Swedish humanist research projects.

Other languages than Greek and Latin were also studied diligently at this period. A literal study of the text of the Bible occupied a central position in the Lutheran faith, and Swedish scholars naturally devoted considerable interest to Hebrew. This interest led on to curiosity about other Semitic languages, notably Arabic. A privately taught nobleman, Johan Gabriel Sparvenfeldt (1655–1725) collected valuable manuscripts, particularly in Arabic, in the course of his extensive travels, but became even more renowned for his knowledge of Slav languages, especially Russian. His impressive Russian–Latin dictionary was never brought out during his lifetime and is only now in the course of publication. Research into Old Norse also began, and Sweden acquired a number of Icelandic manuscripts. This brought new material for the patriotic historiography that was one of the characteristic intellectual endeavours of the period.

Historiography and Gothicism

No account of the learned life of Sweden in the seventeenth century can ignore Gothicism, the school of thought that claimed that the Goths who had once conquered Rome originated from Sweden. This idea, which can be traced at least as far back as the Swedish historians of the late Middle Ages, grew with time into a complex and extensive theoretical structure, well suited to the political ambitions of the new great power and the turgid stylistic ideal of its ruling circles, the Baroque. With the aid of the Icelandic sagas, lists of Swedish kings were constructed that went back to Gog and Magog, the sons of Noah. A bold piece of etymo-

logy, which was typical of seventeenth-century linguistic speculation but had strong roots in the encyclopaedias of the Middle Ages, allowed the word "Gog" to be identified with "Goth", and many other native words to be equated with names from classical literature. The post-classical chronicle of Jordanes on the history of the Goths was not the only source of knowledge of the illustrious ancient history of the Swedes. From ever larger areas of classical literature it proved possible to squeeze material useful in illuminating the heroic exploits of the forefathers. An eager champion of this Gothic reading of the old authorities was the celebrated poet Georg Stiernhielm (1598–1672), who was confident that he could prove that every reference in the ancient sources to that mysterious northern people, the Hyperboreans, fitted Sweden, and that this lent evidence for the view that the country must be heir to one of the oldest and richest cultures on earth. Olaus Verelius (1618–1682), who held a new professorship in Scandinavian antiquities at Uppsala, continued these studies and at the same time strove for a wider knowledge of Old Icelandic literature. But Gothicism reached its peak when his friend Olaus Rudbeck began to make his imaginative contributions to this historiography. With his arrival, it also underwent a partial change of character. In 1679 Rudbeck published the first volume of his *Atlantica*, a work magnificent in conception but never completed, whose title alludes to what he regarded as his own most important historical discovery: that the Atlantis depicted by Plato in the dialogues *Timaios* and *Kritias* was in actual fact Sweden. But this thesis was merely a thread in the tapestry of ambitious historical fantasies that his work presented. Rudbeck attempted to show that Sweden was the first country to be colonized seriously after the Flood and the confusion of tongues, and that it had flourished spiritually and materially before all other countries at this turning point of history, some two thousand years before Christ. From here countless invasions had been launched across the world – the Goths, the earliest inhabitants of Sweden, had founded Troy and left their mark on Babylon and

Rudbeck demonstrates the globe to the sages of antiquity. From Olof Rudbeck the Elder's Atlantica. Uppsala University Library. Photo: Uppsala University Library.

Egypt. And they had introduced the world to astronomy, chronology and the alphabet – the runes in their primitive form were, according to Rudbeck, the oldest of all letters, while chronology and astronomy, of which evidence survived in the runic staffs still used in Rudbeck's time by the common people, were a natural product of the need that arose around the Arctic Circle to keep track of the seasons.

Whereas the entire vision that shines through *Atlantica* (of which part II came out in 1689, part III in 1698 and a fourth, uncompleted part was being printed when Rudbeck died in 1702) forms a gigantic climax to Swedish Gothicism, capable of being understood only as a peculiarly literary expression of the great power ideology that was nourished at this time by the country's political hegemony, the detail work, and in particular the evidential principles, in the *Atlantica* are, paradoxically enough, permeated with the modern scientific spirit that Rudbeck evinced in his other research. What distinguishes the work is not, it must be admitted, rationalist Cartesianism. But in the prodigious chains of evidence that Rudbeck assembles in order to make his theses convincing, there is a great deal of the adherence to empiricism that Francis Bacon – the other philosophical herald of the new spirit – had held up as the essence of the modern programme of research. Rudbeck was surely a Baconian in more senses than one. Naturally, much of his evidence was taken from written sources, the writings of the ancients, as he called them. But in relation to these, too, he adopted a basically empirical attitude. As I myself was not alive at the time, he says, and therefore could not see with my own eyes what happened, I must content myself with what was written on the subject by the ancients, who were there. In fact he goes so far as to lay down rules for the critical evaluation of sources on the basis of their nearness in time and place to the events depicted, uttering cautionary words about the errors and mistakes that may have crept in over the course of time in the narration of what took place. But Rudbeck also adduces evidence of an entirely different type: Sweden's geographical position and form, its landscape of lakes and rivers, stones, animals and plants. Rudbeck compared this landscape in all its diversity with information from the ancient sources on the gardens of the Hesperides, the Elysian Fields, the country of the Hyperboreans and Atlantis, all names that he identified with Sweden – and he succeeded in finding a long series of points of correspondence. He measured the length and breadth of Sweden and found the measurements to agree with those given for Atlantis by Plato in *Timaios*. There was a similar congruence between the capital of Atlantis and Uppsala, as far as the direction of the watercourses, the canals and the dimensions of the walls were concerned. It had all been carefully measured by Rudbeck and reproduced in one of the many maps that illustrated his work. He also carried out extensive archaeological excavations himself, and this at a very early stage in the history of archaeology. Among other things he devised a method of dating burial mounds which is still accepted in its essentials by archaeologists today. He noticed that the surface layer of the soil is augmented every year by a deposit of decaying vegetable matter and by fine particles constantly borne through the air to fall to earth with the rain and snow. Rudbeck observed this rain of particles with the aid of a simple experiment: he placed an open vessel in an outdoor place, sheltered from the wind, and let the winter snow pile up in it. When the snow melted in spring and the meltwater evaporated, there remained a very thin crust of material in the bottom of the vessel. A similar accretion of dust must also be added to the ground everywhere else. By measuring the thickness of this surface layer of the soil, which we now know as humus, at places where the earth had been exposed at a known time in the past, Rudbeck could calculate the annual growth of the layer of humus. By pushing a measuring rod down into the soil to the depth at which a particular find had been discovered, the age of the find could be determined. This is only the most remarkable example of the modern scientific methods employed by Rudbeck in the service of patriotic historiography.

Rudbeck's *Atlantica* attracted international attention,

was reviewed favourably in Pierre Bayle's celebrated *Nouvelles de la république des lettres*, and was criticized but treated seriously by the philosopher Leibniz. In Sweden it was received with enthusiasm, but there were also a number of historians and philologists who opposed the ideas of the *Atlantica* strongly and urged a more cautious and dispassionate archaeology. While the great vision died with the imperial power of Sweden, the spirit which inspired its scientific sections, which lent its strength to the modernist camp during the Cartesian controversies and which slowly spread through the Swedish world of learning in general, formed an inheritance that was put to splendid use by the scientific community of Sweden in the eighteenth century.

References

Eriksson, G., "Olof Rudbeck", *Lychnos* 1984.
Lindborg, R., *Descartes i Uppsala*, Lychnos-Bibliotek 22 (Uppsala 1965).
Lindroth, S., *Svensk lärdomshistoria. Stormaktstiden* (Stockholm, 1975).

Skokloster Castle from Lake Mälar.
Photo: Ulf Leijon

Skokloster – Europe and the World in a Swedish Castle

ARNE LOSMAN

The seventeenth-century Swedish castle of Skokloster, with its remarkable collections of paintings, applied art, furniture, textiles, tools, scientific instruments, weapons and books, constitutes an uncommonly well-preserved monument to Sweden's Age of Greatness. Until quite recent times, the castle has been in private hands. A daughter of the man who had Skokloster built, Carl Gustaf Wrangel, married into the noble house of Brahe, and the castle remained in that family until 1930. It then became the property of the barons von Essen until it was bought by the Swedish government in 1967. This facilitated the necessary restoration of the building and a more systematic care and scientific management of the collections.

Skokloster was seen as a museum even in the eighteenth century. It was looked on as a memorial to its celebrated builder and to a departed age of Swedish imperial power. Rather later – early in the nineteenth century – the castle and its collections were regarded more as a kind of national museum. The early evolution of this view of Skokloster as a memorial and a museum is one of the main reasons for the preservation of the castle in a relatively unaltered state.

Today Skokloster is a museum enjoyed by large numbers of Swedish and foreign visitors, including many from the United States. The castle gives an evocative recapitulation of important aspects of the history of Sweden in the seventeenth century. Skokloster is a microcosm – physically and metaphysically – of an age which believed the world could be mirrored in a model.

The Building of the Castle

The waters of Mälaren have reflected the castle of Skokloster since 1668. Sweden's third largest lake has here a deep inlet that forms a part of the waterway between the capital, Stockholm, and the old university city of Uppsala, a waterway that was much more important in the seventeenth century than it is today. In the year mentioned, a dozen bricklayers and their forty or so labourers laid the last eighty thousand bricks. Sweden's largest great residence – with the exception of the palaces of the monarch – was externally complete, a four-storey building in the form of an open square, with octagonal towers at the outer corners. At the time, the huge castle of St. Johannisburg in the Bavarian town of Aschaffenburg was mentioned as a model. But there are greater architectural similarities with another castle from earlier in the seventeenth century, the Ujazdow of the Swedish-Polish King Sigismund in Warsaw.

Work on the building of the castle had been in progress since 1654, with breaks for winter. It was a period of many harsh winters. During the Danish War, for example, the Swedish armies under Karl X Gustav were able to cross the ice of the Little Belt and the Great Belt in January and February 1658 and thus force Denmark to accept the very severe Treaty of Roskilde. A leading part in this military campaign was played by the then count, field-marshal and admiral of the realm Carl Gustaf Wrangel (1613–1676), the man who, four years earlier, had ordered work to start on the building of Skokloster.

The exterior of Skokloster was thus completed be-

The unfinished banqueting hall. Skokloster Castle.
Photo: Sören Hallgren

tween 1654 and 1668. Work on the interior continued for several decades more. But some of the eighty rooms in the palace were never finished. The great banqueting hall, 3,500 sq. ft. in area, and the finest guest chambers nearby are unfinished and undecorated even today. The banqueting hall was planned for the kind of merry-making that delighted Wrangel and his contemporaries, feasts of culinary abundance involving the ceremonial consumption of up to six hundred dishes and torrents of wine with the assistance of artists, poets, musicians and pyrotechnicists. Such banquets – the great artistic creations of the Baroque – were arranged at other Wrangel residences but not in the great hall at Skokloster. This stands instead as if in a time warp, a frozen moment of seventeenth-century Swedish history, a building site where the echo of the foreman's last order has barely died away and where the mason's clinking trowel and the carpenter's banging hammer have just this minute fallen silent. The people have left the rooms. Their tools are still there. Nearer than this to the toils and skills of the hard-working artisans of three hundred years ago we cannot come.

The unfinished banqueting hall also has a close connection with the domestic Swedish politics of the 1680s, with the inquiry into the administration of the regency and the reduction (repossession of landed estates by the Crown), described elsewhere in this volume by Sven A. Nilsson. Enormous dues were demanded by the government from the Wrangel estate, and Wrangel's heirs were barely able to keep and maintain the castle. In this way the castle became a symbol of the massive exertions of the Age of Greatness, a time of grandiose projects that could not always be carried through. Skokloster is also a manifestation of other essential features of seventeenth-century Sweden, such as the close dependence on the rest of Europe and the growing collaboration with this world beyond Sweden's shores, a process which is sometimes known as the country's Europeanization and which has deep roots in the previous century.

Let us consider this in concrete terms. From where,

for example, were the building materials for Skokloster obtained? The bricks came, it is true, from local brickyards. Iron was supplied by ironworks relatively near at hand and copper came from the Falun mine in Dalarna. But lime and sandstone were brought from Gotland. Oak was shipped across the sea from Pomerania and the Baltic territories. The glass for the windows also came from Pomerania. The black-glazed roof tiles were purchased from Amsterdam, from where also was shipped the Italian marble that adorns the portico of the building.

The people who erected the castle also came from far and wide. The digging of the foundations was begun by

Four men of Dalarna.
Lorenzo Magalotti, Relazione di Svezia 1674.
Manuscript in the Uppsala University Library.
Photo: Uppsala University Library.

thirty men from Dalarna in 1654. From then on, the heaviest work was done by soldiers and – not least – by women, the "lime stirrers". From well-preserved accounts we know quite a lot about the names of the workers and their social and financial conditions. What surprises us most is perhaps that the threat of a strike was already in the air by 1655. The soldiers protested when they discovered that the women were receiving a rather higher daily wage than theirs. The threat to strike was effective. The overseer raised the soldiers' wages to the level of the women's, although this led the future proprietor – less surprisingly – to write expressing his displeasure.

Before long, stonemasons, stuccoworkers, decorators, landscape gardeners and other specialists were needed. The accounts tell of men from Pomerania, Hessen and Italy. Without the know-how of these Continental craftsmen, Skokloster could not have been built. Behind them we discern the architects, among whom may be included the owner himself, his drive and authority making up for the amateur nature of his architectural knowledge. But there were also such men as Caspar Vogel from Erfurt in Germany, Nicodemus Tessin the Elder from Pomerania and Jean De la Vallée, son of the immigrant French architect Simon De la Vallée.

On 1 October 1663, Wrangel drew up a contract with the stuccoworkers H. Zauch and J.A. Anthoni. The two craftsmen, of German and Italian origin respectively, were to produce a stucco ceiling for the great dining hall of Skokloster and two adjoining rooms. The dining hall, which began in the mid-eighteenth century to be known as the King's Hall, was given a magnificent ceiling in deep relief. In the corners there are large medallions, bearing symbolic images of the continents of Europe, Africa, Asia and America (the last-named showing an Indian girl with an armadillo). In the centre of the ceiling we see a mythological figure struggling with a dragon; presumably these are Apollo and Python. Both Louis XIV in France and Karl XI in Sweden were glorified as the dragon-slaying Apollo. We do not know how Wrangel interpreted the imagery of the ceiling, but he was probably not averse to seeing himself, or at least imperial Sweden, as the centre of the world.

But at the same time the ceiling of Skokloster's King's Hall expresses Sweden's lessening dependence on other countries. In 1672 a glass chandelier was fixed to the dragon's jaws. Since then, it has hung undisturbed for more than three hundred years. It was made at a Stockholm glassworks which was managed by a Swede, Melchior Jung. This glassworks had begun operations in the reign of Queen Christina, with the aid of Italian glassblowers. But by the 1660s, when the works provided a livelihood for forty families, all the employees were Swedes. With evident pride Jung reports this fact in a letter to the government. As a whole, Skokloster tells of the import of luxuries by the titled nobility. But the white, blue, yellow and red glass of the chandelier also reflects how the domestic manufacture of such items was starting to grow. This development is discussed in the article by Margareta Revera which follows.

The Proprietor

Every man is a piece of the Continent, a part of the main. John Donne's words can certainly be applied to the builder of Skokloster, Carl Gustaf Wrangel, a man who was more European than Swedish and in that respect a typical member of the seventeenth-century Swedish aristocracy.

Wrangel was born in 1613 in an earlier manor house at Skokloster. This smaller building still stands beside the great castle today, an illustration of the relatively modest capabilities and ambitions of the era of Gustav II Adolf.

His father was a soldier of Estonian extraction, who received the estate of Skokloster in 1611 as a donation from the Crown. This Herman Wrangel later rose to be a field-marshal and died in Riga in 1643 as the newly appointed governor-general of Livonia. He was buried in

The ceiling of the King's Hall, with the glass chandelier. Skokloster. Photo: Sören Hallgren

Medallion bearing symbolic image of the continent of America. Skokloster. Photo: Sören Hallgren

Medallion bearing symbolic image of the continent of Europe. Skokloster. Photo: Sören Hallgren

Detail of equestrian portrait of Carl Gustaf Wrangel by D.K. Ehrenstrahl, 1652. Skokloster.
Photo: Skokloster.

a new memorial chapel in the church at Skokloster. Since the Reformation this church has been a Lutheran parish church and has also served as the palace chapel. But it was originally built for "Sko kloster", a medieval nunnery of the Cistercian order. Skokloster Church reminds us of a time when Sweden's cultural contacts with the rest of the Europe took place under the auspices of the Roman Catholic Church and the monastic orders.

Carl Gustaf Wrangel's mother, Margareta Grip, belonged to a noble Swedish family of long standing. Her son received the upbringing and the education which were customary in this social class. In other words, he went through a well-rounded programme of moral and physical education that has its roots in Italian Renaissance humanism. It is a programme that is summarized on the facade of the Palace of the Nobility in Stockholm, and in particular by the pithy expression *Arte et Marte* (by Art and War). (The Palace of the Nobility is referred to in greater detail in the contributions of Allan Ellenius and Margareta Revera to this volume.)

Around 1630, Carl Gustaf Wrangel made the Continental grand tour customary among the titled nobility and studied for some time at the University of Leiden in the Netherlands. He also visited a school for the nobility in Paris, i.e. a school of the type that laid the emphasis on certain military subjects, such as fortifications science and fencing, in combination with dancing, modern languages and other accomplishments intended to create a man of the world, or – to use the French term of the day – a *gentil-homme*. Shortly before the battle of Lützen in 1632, at which Gustav II Adolf was killed, Wrangel began serving with the Swedish forces in Germany. This was the start of a career of rapid promotions, even though one of his superiors, the Swedish general John Banér, took strong exception to what he considered Wrangel's French affectations. Although he never again visited France, Wrangel is an early example of a Gallicized Swedish nobleman. French, like Swedish and German, was a language of which he had a thorough command.

Wrangel's reputation first reached Europe in 1644, when he led a united Swedish and chartered Dutch fleet to victory over a Danish fleet off Femern on the German coast. In 1646 he became field-marshal and commander-in-chief of the Swedish forces in Germany. As such, he co-operated during the final stages of the Thirty Years' War with the French, represented by the celebrated General Turenne. Wrangel was in high favour with Queen Christina and as the peace treaty was concluded he received many estates and large sums of money, together with nomination to the post of governor-general of the Swedish province of Pomerania in northern Germany. Somewhat later he also became a count, with a countship at Salmis, near Lake Ladoga at the eastern limit of Sweden's then possessions.

There were many matters to be settled after the Treaty of Westphalia, such as paying off the armies that had fought in the war. These were discussed at the great congress which took place at Nuremberg in 1649–1650 and in which representatives of the three powers of Sweden, France and the German Empire participated. Wrangel threw himself whole-heartedly into the conference, which lasted almost a year, and while he was there he met a host of poets, musicians, artists and actors from different countries.

Wrangel had already begun to build up a court circle of his own during the long war and had, for example, engaged the eminent artist Matthaus Merian the Younger from Frankfurt am Main as his court painter. In the early 1650s he began to increase his efforts in this direction while governor-general of Pomerania, where he lived in the former ducal castles of Stettin and Wolgast and built great houses of his own such as the luxurious country seat of Wrangelsburg. It was here in Pomerania that the young David Klöcker, later ennobled as Ehrenstrahl, began his career as painter to the Wrangelian court, one of his first works being the large equestrian portrait of Wrangel in 1652, which now hangs at Skokloster.

In addition to his duties in Pomerania, Wrangel – now Count Wrangel – held high office for the rest of his life in the government of Sweden, including membership of the regency of Karl XI, first as admiral of the realm and later as marshal of the realm. He also held high military command in further wars, such as those against Poland and Denmark in 1655–1660. Finally, in 1674, he was a driving force behind the decision to invade Brandenburg, a disaster for Sweden and a fiasco for Wrangel personally.

The greater part of the life work of this aristocrat consisted in leading armies and fleets in war. But there were peaceful interludes. The longest was between 1661 and 1673, when Wrangel did not take part in any armed conflict except for a blockade of the German free city of Bremen in 1666. He spent a large part of this period of peace in Pomerania, where he lived almost as a North German prince. He took a deep interest in the intellectual life of the province, and was chancellor of the University of Greifswald. Sometimes he visited Continental spas and took part in their social life. On several occasions he visited Hamburg, where he met ex-Queen Christina, who had travelled up from Rome. From time to time Wrangel was in Sweden proper, usually in Stockholm, where his big palace on Riddarholmen (today occupied by the Svea Court of Appeal) was being furnished and decorated at the same time as similar work was being done at Skokloster.

Wrangel had been married since 1640 to the German-born Anna Margareta von Haugwitz (1622–1673). Most of their eleven children died in childhood; only three daughters survived Wrangel. During his continuous peregrinations he was always accompanied by his family and also by a large retinue, which included secretaries, chaplains, cooks and musicians.

Wrangel and Europe

Knowledge is power. This maxim was equally true in the seventeenth century. Wrangel needed knowledge for his role as soldier, politician and landed proprietor. He also needed it while assembling his symbols of power: the many great houses with their collections of art and other objects contributing to the festive atmosphere of his court. In part this knowledge consisted of information on the swings of fashion, which were important in the competition for social status, i.e. the endeavour to create ceremonial surroundings that were as splendid as, and preferably a little more so than, the other aristocratic courts within and outside Sweden's borders.

How did a man like Wrangel obtain his comprehensive information, other than from his own observations and personal conversation? His news media were letters, newspapers and books, which he received from a number of people living in various parts of Europe: news agents, trade commissioners, Sweden's diplomatic representatives. From Hamburg, Amsterdam, The Hague and London, he received in the 1660s at least one letter a week containing political, military, commercial and cultural news.

Printed newspapers were often enclosed in these letters. In the course of Wrangel's lifetime European newspaper publishing grew from virtually nothing to roughly fifty papers, published in some thirty different places. Wrangel took a number of them, reading, for example, the book advertisements of the Dutch papers and ordering new books on the strength of them.

In order to bring out more clearly the way in which Wrangel's foreign contacts worked – and thereby demonstrate part of the mechanism underlying the process of Europeanization – two of these men will be mentioned here: Peter Trotzig in Amsterdam and Johan Leijonbergh in London. Both were Swedes and corresponded with Wrangel in Swedish, a point worth emphasizing, as the vast majority of the fifty thousand or so surviving letters to and from Wrangel are in German. For several decades, these two men served both the Swedish state and a number of aristocrats, Trotzig as a trade commissioner and Leijonbergh as a permanent diplomatic representative, or "resident".

It was Peter Trotzig who arranged the deliveries of Dutch glazed tiles for the roof of Skokloster. He sent detailed weekly reports on various novelties and enclosed newspapers from Amsterdam and Haarlem. He also helped Wrangel to buy a wide range of goods intended to enrich and beautify the setting in which Wrangel would extend hospitality and parade his social status: tapestries, gilt-leather wall hangings, the latest books, coaches, weapons for the armoury, scientific instruments, tools for the count's joinery workshop and turnery (Wrangel was one of the first aristocrats in Sweden to treat woodworking as a noble art). At the same time Trotzig supplied similar items to other members of the nobles' Estate, such as the politically more eminent Magnus Gabriel De la Gardie, who was also on Karl XI's regency council and a successful rival of Wrangel for status.

The resident in London, Johan Leijonbergh, was a well-informed man, who not only kept Wrangel acquainted with events at the English court, fleet movements in the English Channel, the great plague of 1665 and the fire of London in 1666. He was also in a position to pass on information on innovations in science and technology, being the first Swedish member of the Royal Society and an associate of such men as Samuel Pepys. He had a sharp ear for the topics of debate in these circles, as in 1662 when John Evelyn discussed the dearth of forest timber. Sweden had similar problems of reckless forest felling around the mines and ironworks. The country was also short of oak for the needs of the navy. Leijonbergh tried – although without conspicuous success – to interest Wrangel, as admiral of the realm, in reforestation. Wrangel showed a greater interest in the manufacture of sophisticated telescopes and microscopes that was taking place in the London of the 1660s, and through Leijonbergh he purchased several. He shared an interest in modern science and technology with many aristocrats. Although these powerful figures possessed only a superficial knowledge in such fields, they must nevertheless have contributed to a flow of scientific information to imperial Sweden.

Wrangel in the World of Books

In the early stages of the Thirty Years' War, the German city of Heidelberg was taken by the imperial general, Tilly. The city's immense library, *Bibliotheca Palatina*, which was known to contemporaries as the mother of libraries, was carried off to Rome, where it was incorporated in the library of the Vatican. The Swedes, too, gathered the literary spoils of war. This is one of the reasons for the dynamic growth of Swedish libraries in the seventeenth century, as illustrated by the library of Uppsala University during the reign of Gustav II Adolf. Of later monarchs, Queen Christina showed a marked interest in acquiring books as war booty and obtained many from Prague. As well as benefitting the large public libraries – which include the important libraries of the *gymnasia* – the acquisitions also enriched many private collections, not least those in the stately homes of the nobility.

In this respect, too, Carl Gustaf Wrangel is very typical. Part of his library is plunder, even if the majority of it was acquired by other means. He left a collection of 2,400 volumes, a comparatively large number by contemporary standards. But this was far exceeded by the eight thousand or so volumes making up the library of Magnus Gabriel De la Gardie, the greatest Swedish bibliophile – with the exception of the monarchs – of the seventeenth century. The cultural ideal of the aristocracy called for universality, which is clearly reflected in the libraries of Wrangel and other magnates. Modern research is greatly assisted when libraries have come down to us untouched, as they then give us an insight into the whole intellectual landscape in which these influential persons moved. In Wrangel's case, a representative selection – about a quarter – of his books has been preserved at Skokloster. The entire collection can be reconstructed from surviving catalogues, book orders and booksellers' invoices. Today his books are kept in one of the seven rooms of the library on the top floor of Skokloster, together with the personal libraries of other important sixteenth, seventeenth and eighteenth century aristocrats.

Interior view of part of the library at Skokloster.
Photo: Ulf Leijon

Wrangel acquired his books in many different ways. War booty has already been referred to. Other books came to him by inheritance or as gifts. Men of learning would often send copies of their latest works in the hope that this would further their career. Scholars from the University of Greifswald and masters at the *gymnasium* in Stettin, the provincial capital of Pomerania, did so. At the same time, Wrangel was always buying books himself. Purchases from Holland in response to newspaper advertisements have already been mentioned. Large quantities were bought direct from booksellers in Hamburg. And from the publishing house of Merian in Frankfurt am Main he bought the current chronicles *Theatrum Europaeum*, to which he himself contributed material in order to keep his name in the public eye.

The wide-ranging library of an aristocratic universalist such as Wrangel covered every conceivable subject field from theology to technology. Within theology, many faiths were represented. Wrangel had syncretic sympathies: he was not opposed to what we would today call ecumenicalism. In this he differed from his fellow nobles such as Per Brahe, the lord high steward, who feared that any departure from Lutheran ortodoxy might bring political unrest and division.

As a patron of architects, Wrangel naturally possessed a good deal of literature on architecture, by such authorities as the Italians Palladio, Serlio and Vignola; the Frenchmen Barbet, Delorme, Ducerceau and the landscape gardener appointed by Queen Christina, André Mollet; the Dutchmen J. van Campen and Vingboons; and the Germans Böckler and Furttenbach. The science of the century was represented by works of astronomy by Galileo and Hevelius.

French belles-lettres and drama were much in evidence, with such names as Mme de Lafayette, Mlle de Scudéry, Corneille and Molière.

The enumeration of authors need not be continued, especially as there is no way of knowing how many of the books the owner had actually read. But the many descriptions of travels in foreign lands must be mentioned – Wrangel's interest in what were to Europeans exotic countries is very apparent. In this context it may be appropriate to note Kircher's book on China, printed in 1667, particularly as Wrangel was to buy tea from Amsterdam in 1673 and thus become the first known Swedish tea importer. This event is a mark both of the Swedish aristocracy's dawning enthusiasm for China and of its taste for fashionable new luxuries.

America and New Sweden

The aristocracy's interest in distant lands is apparent everywhere to the visitor who makes a tour of the collections. The very material of the various *objets d'art* tells us this: fine cabinets of ivory and ebony; plates, mirror frames and bookbindings of tortoiseshell; goblets and ornaments made out of rhinoceros horn and ostrich eggs.

Naturally the owner of Skokloster was also fascinated by America. We have already seen a symbolic expression of this in the stucco ceiling of the King's Hall. From Holland he obtained a painting of Brazilian parrots. He was able to read the history of Brazil under Dutch sovereignty in the years around 1640 in Caspar Barlaeus' voluminous work on the subject (Amsterdam, 1647). Descriptions of travels in the West Indies were also a prominent feature of the collection. And he was able to form a different, less factual impression of America – a sort of American romanticism – as a participant in some of the festivities of the Swedish court, where the aristocracy used to amuse themselves by dressing up as Indians.

Nor was Wrangel indifferent to American enjoyments. He bought Virginian tobacco through the aforementioned Peter Trotzig of Amsterdam, and in 1670 he began to buy Mexican cocoa, which reached him at Skokloster by way of Amsterdam, Hamburg and Stockholm. This made him not only Sweden's first known tea drinker but also its first consumer of chocolate.

Carl Gustaf Wrangel's father, Herman Wrangel, was one of those who on 15 August 1642 signed the instruc-

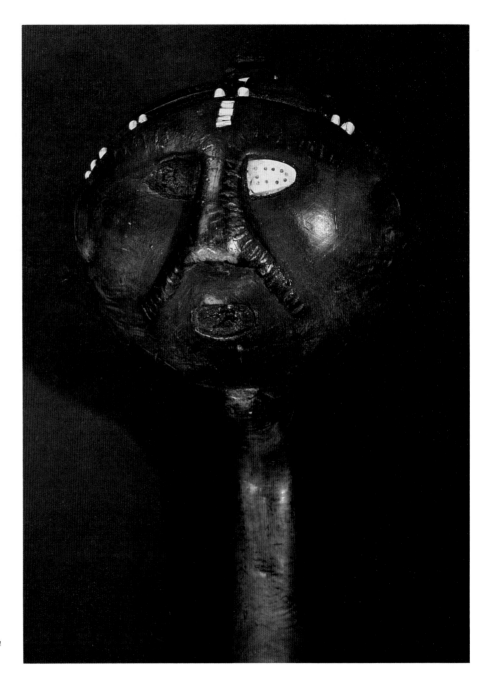

Indian club. From
Wrangel's armoury.
Skokloster.
Photo: Samuel Uhrdin

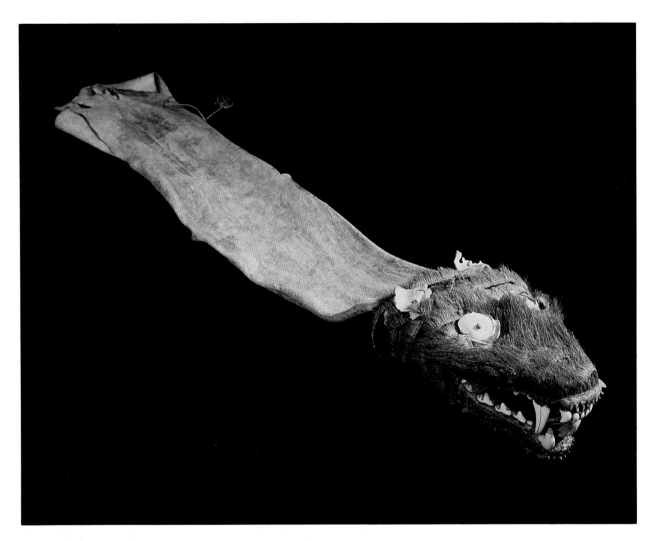

Indian wolf's head.
From Wrangel's armou-
ry. Skokloster.
Photo: Samuel Uhrdin

tions to Johan Printz, the governor of New Sweden from 1643 to 1653. Carl Gustaf Wrangel showed no great commitment to the Delaware project. In this, too, the builder of Skokloster was fairly typical of the Swedish aristocracy, who were, as Margareta Revera relates below, lukewarm about the venture. But naturally Wrangel, who was always well informed, was aware of developments in New Sweden.

This may be illustrated from his correspondence, with a letter that he received while encamped in Germany in March 1646. The writer was Trotzig, who said that he had been away from Amsterdam for some time. The reason was, said Trotzig, that as the agent of the Swedish crown he had been occupied in "fitting out Nova Sveica, which in this country must proceed in silence on account of the West India Company". With this, Wrangel was given a glimpse of the difficulties of a Swedish commercial agent working for the New Sweden Company in the shadow of Holland's powerful West India Company.

Let us conclude by taking a tour of the top floor of Skokloster, which includes the three rooms housing Wrangel's armoury. Here the proprietor accumulated large numbers of weapons, chiefly richly decorated hunting pieces. At the same time it was from the very start a kind of museum, to some extent resembling the *Kunst- und Wunderkammer* on the Continent. There are, for example, a great many ethnographical items from different countries, among them a hammock from Latin America. But the attention of our American visitors is most frequently attracted by a chest containing eight Indian artefacts, which are presumed to originate from along the lower reaches of the Delaware.

These artefacts have many times been mentioned in the literature, together with the traditional information that Wrangel received them as a gift from Johan Printz, the governor of New Sweden who was referred to earlier. However, this is not corroborated by letter or in any other form, and there is room for speculation. As they are first recorded as belonging to the Wrangelian armoury as late as 1710, we cannot even be sure that Wrangel was the first Swedish owner.

If Wrangel really did own these objects, there are a number of ways in which he could have acquired them. He may have bought them in Holland. He may have received them as gifts, perhaps from his colleague in the regency Per Brahe, who is known to have received items of ethnographic interest from Printz. Wrangel was also in touch with other Swedes who had served in the colony and may have supplied him with Indian artefacts. A work on economics published in 1669 by Johan Rising, Printz' successor as governor of New Sweden, is to be found among Wrangel's books, with a handwritten dedication.

What is more interesting is his contact with another traveller to America, Per Lindeström, well-known for his description of a journey to New Sweden in 1653–1656, which was presented to the young Prince Karl, the future Karl XII, in 1691. Lindeström's map of New Sweden is reliably reported to have been in the library at Skokloster in 1709, but unfortunately it has since disappeared. It is said to have borne a dedication from Lindeström to Wrangel, dated 1666.

In his castle of Skokloster and its contents, Carl Gustaf Wrangel tried to create a microcosm of the world. This did not omit the New World.

References

Andrén, Erik, *Skokloster. Ett slottsbygge under stormaktstiden* (Building a castle in imperial Sweden) (Stockholm, 1948).

Andrén, Erik, "Melchior Jungs glasbruk i Stockholm 1641–1678" (Melchior Jung's glassworks in Stockholm, 1641–1678) in *Samfundet S:t Eriks Årsbok 1972/73*.

Eimer, Gerhard, *Carl Gustaf Wrangel som byggherre i Pommern och Sverige* (Carl Gustaf Wrangel as a builder in Pomerania and Sweden) (Stockholm, 1961).

Losman, Arne, *Carl Gustaf Wrangel och Europa. Studier i kulturförbindelser kring en 1600-talsmagnat* Carl Gustaf Wrangel and Europe. Studies in the cultural communications network of a seventeenth century magnate). Studies and sources published by the Swedish History of Science Society Nr 33 (Stockholm, 1980).

"Life at court."
From Hortus Regius, *by*
Schering Rosenhane. Royal
Swedish Library.
Photo: Royal Swedish
Library.

The Making of a Civilized Nation. Nation-Building, Aristocratic Culture and Social Change

MARGARETA REVERA

The ostentatious extravagance of the seventeenth-century Swedish aristocracy is in many ways a highly charged story. It always has been – there was from the outset an underlying purpose in the luxurious living that was so characteristic of the social elite in the Swedish Age of Greatness. That this luxuriousness can still be enthralling is something that I shall try to show by describing the transformation of Sweden from a relatively backward agrarian society on the fringe of Europe into a civilized nation.

The new aristocratic lifestyle, various aspects of which have already been illuminated by the contributions of Allan Ellenius and Arne Losman to this volume, was, like so much else in seventeenth-century Sweden, an import. With its origins in the European courtly culture of the late Renaissance it was intimately associated with the growth of the strong new nation states of early modern Europe, and when it belatedly took root in Sweden it did so in the context of the country's newly attained great-power status and the nation-building that was taking place, initially under the energetic leadership of Gustav II Adolf and Axel Oxenstierna. This building of a nation, against the background of the overshadowing dictates of military policy and war-financing and in an underpopulated country with a comparatively undeveloped economy, has been described and analysed by Sven A. Nilsson in the first of the essays in this volume. The intellectual backwardness of Sweden has been thought-provokingly underlined by Gunnar Eriksson, who notes the absence in Sweden of the kinds of association which formed the centres of modern science elsewhere in Europe, i.e. new academies or societies of representatives of commerce, engineering and politics. Bodies of this kind did not appear in Sweden until the first half of the eighteenth century, by which time Sweden had managed to cut back the lead of more advanced nations in other respects as well. The most eye-catching change had been in the architectural environment, where after decades of intensive building activity the royal family and the aristocracy could now parade such residences as Drottningholm, the Palace of the Nobility in Stockholm and Skokloster, while many merchants had built "great houses of stone" of the kind that Gustav II Adolf had wished to see replace their "little cabins", as he expressed it in a well-known address to the *riksdag* in 1630 before Sweden's entry into the German war. Furthermore, Sweden had by now developed from being very much an importer of both scholarship and art to a level where the flow was also in the other direction. By this time, the period of great-power status had come to an end, together with nearly forty years of monarchic absolutism, another European phenomenon that was late in reaching Sweden. And the Age of Greatness had given way to the Era of Liberty.

Together with the role of the aristocratic lifestyle in this process, my essay will also consider New Sweden, the 350th anniversary of whose founding we are celebrating this year. A Swedish professor of history observed in connection with the tercentenary in 1938 that hardly any chapter of Sweden's seventeenth-century history can have been so thoroughly investigated as the short-lived colonial venture in America and its background, a subject which, he nevertheless considered, had to be regarded as somewhat peripheral to the main events. It is easy to agree with his first assertion, bearing in mind the enormous literature on New Sweden on both sides of the Atlantic, but his second today appears anything but accurate. The knowledge of seventeenth-century Sweden that we now possess makes the New Sweden enterprise very interesting indeed, provided that it is put in its correct context. This is a context which also has to include the lifestyle of the aristocracy, however unexpected this may sound.

Myths and Traditions

It may well seem that hardly any other epoch in Swedish history has been so "thoroughly investigated" as the Age of Greatness, which is of course no guarantee that its correct context has been brought to light. The aristocratic lifestyle of the Age of Greatness and its place in the social transformation that took place at that time are, however, a subject more cocooned in myth than investigated, one which has entirely failed to excite the interest of recent historians. One undoubted reason for this is that the spendthrift excesses of the seventeenth-century nobility have been regarded as having obstructed social progress. It is with this myth-enveloped and "reprehensible" extravagance that this essay is primarily concerned.

The myths surrounding this extravagance are old. On closer examination they are by no means uninteresting, but as they have gone unquestioned they have had an unfortunate influence on later research, leading to the decidedly misleading picture of the seventeenth-century aristocractic lifestyle that has been propagated in both serious and popular accounts. Among the hardiest of these myths is the claim that it was the young Count Magnus Gabriel De la Gardie who brought extravagant fashions to Sweden, which he is supposed to have done when he returned from his embassy to France in 1647. He is reported, for example, to have impressed his guests at a dazzling banquet by providing the cutlery for them all (the custom was for guests to bring their own), in a display of household affluence never before seen in Sweden.

De la Gardie's reputation as the main introducer of luxurious living is part of a tradition that pinpoints the reign of Christina as the time when ostentatious extravagance began to appear and which emphasizes that this coincided with the end of the war, the donations of landed estates to the aristocracy and, last but by no means least, the rise of a new generation within the aristocracy. With this younger generation of aristocrats – the newly rich successors of the war veterans of the 1630s – a new culture is supposed to have arrived, characterized by a new way of life that was also adopted by the remainder of the nobility as far as their means allowed. Uncouth habits were thus replaced by elegant manners, it has been said, and an important role in the rapid spread of the new lifestyle of the upper class is ascribed to Queen Christina – her hectic and expensive amusements are said to have set the fashion. It is also customary to say that the new mansions of the nobility were built with German money and filled with war booty. The most celebrated collection of war booty is also claimed to have opened Swedish eyes to the country's extreme cultural backwardness. This is a reference to the looting of Prague, which was taken in the very final stages of the Thirty Years' War in 1648, with its fantastic literary and artistic riches. The Silver Bible from the imperial collections (now in the Uppsala University Library) and the bronze sculptures by Adriaen de Vries from the gardens of General Wallenstein's mansion (now in the gardens of Drottningholm Palace) are among the priceless treasures brought over to Sweden.

The idea of a change of generation is the most important strand in this tradition. It dates back to a nineteenth-century school of political and cultural historiography that was highly critical of the aristocratic regency of Karl XI from 1660-1672 (in which De la Gardie was chancellor) and depicted the nobility as uniformly degenerate or at least verging on decadence. A decadence that is taken to have contributed to the unhappy events that ensued, i.e. the commission of inquiry into the regency, the reduction (repossession of landed estates by

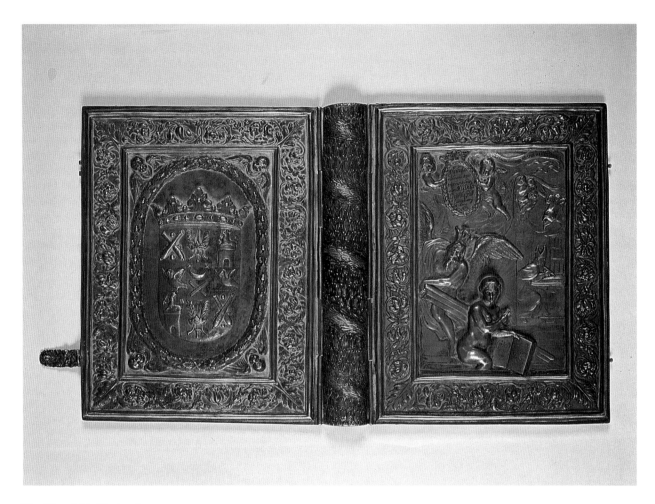

The Silver Bible (Codex Argenteus). *Uppsala University Library.*
Photo: Uppsala University Library.

the Crown), the fall of the aristocracy constituting the council of the realm, and monarchic absolutism. Nor were the strictest moralists in any doubt about why and when the decline set in. The cause was the foreign aristocratic culture – the luxury and the refinement – imported by De la Gardie and others of his generation, whose lifestyle is described as one marked by prodigality, a craving for luxuries and a general "lack of public spirit". The whole period is sharply contrasted with the simplicity of the previous regency (1632-1644), and with the "first generation" of aristocrats in the Age of Greatness, normally represented by Axel Oxenstierna and his political acumen, love of country, lack of self-seeking and, of course, distaste for any form of luxury. Such a judgment on the ills of the age was passed as early as 1675 by Per Brahe, the ageing steward of the realm, who had been a member of both regencies.

In its present-day form the tradition has changed to the extent that the moralizing has disappeared, and with it the condemnation of the extravagance, but the emphasis on a generation gap remains, and Magnus Gabriel De la Gardie is sometimes cited as evidence of its existence. This is because, interestingly enough, the belief that it was De la Gardie who brought the taste for extravagance to Sweden agrees with the chancellor's own view of the matter, recorded for posterity by the Italian diplomat Lorenzo Magalotti in his Swedish travel diaries of 1674.

Whereas Magalotti was so impressed by the luxury of the Stockholm of the 1670s that he portrayed the Swedish capital as a French colony, his compatriot, Marquis Alessandro Bichi, saw no cause for similar eulogies just over twenty years later. On the contrary, his travel journal dated 1696 has been quoted as support for the widely held view that the luxurious living died out towards the end of the Age of Greatness, by which time only vestiges of the old splendour survived. Underlying this view of matters is the notion that the aristocracy was crushed by the upheavals of the 1680s and that the men of the period of Caroline absolutism were for the most part a crowd of uncultivated upstarts, a myth ema-

nating originally from the opponents of the reduction and of absolutism among the old titled nobility. As Bichi himself relates, his guide in Stockholm was in fact a member of this latter group.

In other words, the tradition of a clearly demarcated age of luxury consumption rests on an unsure foundation. Many accounts contain contradictions and it is evident that the theory of a change of generation has tended to obscure, for example, the existence of luxurious housing in and around the Stockholm of the 1630s, glimpses of which are seen in the diary of Charles Ogier, the secretary of the French legation in 1634-35. Prominence has instead been given to those settings that did not find favour with the Frenchman, which have been used to justify talk of a still prevailing simplicity. When this is remembered, we are no longer surprised at the contradictory nature of the contention that the trendsetter in luxury consumption, De la Gardie, appearing in his new French attire in Munnichhoven's portrait of the early 1650s, is displaying a singular contempt for all prohibitions of extravagance, by which is meant the sumptuary ordinances. In other words there was already an awareness of an extravagance so widespread as to necessitate legislation for its restraint.

But there is not a lot about this in the literature, nor has the luxury of the final decades of the Age of Greatness been adequately researched. This is a result of the myths surrounding the subject, which must not of course be taken at their word. The interesting thing about them is, rather, what they imply about the function of the consumption of luxuries; that De la Gardie should have boasted to an impressed foreigner of having brought luxury to Sweden provokes a number of reflections. The striking interest of foreigners in Swedish homes, festivities and mode of dress is an expression of their concern with one question: Sweden was indeed a great power, but was she also a civilized nation? And it is the foreigners who tell of the war booty, in reports that are not infrequently tendentious. As one of the more innocent examples, mention may be made of Bulstrode Whitelocke, Cromwell's ambassador to

Count Magnus Gabriel De la Gardie and his wife Maria Euphrosyne of Pfalz-Zweibrücken. Painting by Hendrick Munnichhoven, 1653. Gripsholm Palace. Photo: Swedish Portrait Archives.

Sweden in 1653-54, who noted a particularly costly silver dish at a banquet given by Erik Oxenstierna and assumed it to be plunder from Germany, whereas it was in all probability a wedding present from Estonia, where Oxenstierna had been governor. That the Swedes did not lack insight into the function of a display of extravagance is clear from Per Brahe's attitude when he was criticized by his father for his expenditure while studying abroad in the years around 1620. Brahe defended his purchases of clothing on the grounds that it was not enough to have a roof over one's head if one was to keep up appearances among foreigners. In the story of luxury consumption, the new lifestyle and aristocratic culture in Sweden this is a more telling episode than the same man's jeremiad, more than fifty years later, on the wastefulness of the younger generation.

Since the nineteenth-century denunciations of the extravagance of the Age of Greatness, the subject has hardly attracted the attention of any historian. One notable exception, however, is Eli Heckscher, the economic historian of international repute, who made his classic attempt at a broad survey of Swedish seventeenth-century society in the 1930s. Heckscher, too, was critical of the extravagance, but for the reason that the enormous increase in expenditure on consumption prevented saving and productive investment. Being unimpressed by the change-of-generation theory, however, he put the start of the aristocracy's extravagance in the latter part of the sixteenth century. Other facets of the picture of an antiquated and non-dynamic agrarian seventeenth-century society, as presented by Heckscher, are the emphasis on the payment of taxes in kind and the barter economy, and also the traditional belief that the rule of the aristocracy delayed agricultural development until the threat to peasant freedom had been removed by the great reduction. To this has to be added the drop in the living standards of the broad strata of the population, which in Heckscher's opinion occurred during the seventeenth century as a result of the great-power policy and the nobility's heavy taxation of the peasantry. As, what is more, luxury goods such as wines and superior textiles for the exclusive enjoyment of the small elite were a significant part of the country's imports at the end of the seventeenth century, just as they had been at the beginning, Heckscher states that the seventeenth century, "continued in all its essentials to rest on the foundations of the old economy".

In these circumstances, it is understandable that the transformation of Swedish society is usually seen as having started in the eighteenth century. Foreign historians who have considered events in Sweden from an international perspective have also pointed out the slow pace of development, particularly by comparison with England. A similar attitude to the chronology of development (but only to its chronology) was expressed by one of Sweden's nineteenth-century cultural historians, who thought she saw in the enthusiasm of the early part of the Era of Liberty for industry and science – for the building of factories and the establishment of trading companies and for the Royal Swedish Academy of Sciences that was founded in 1739 – a counterpart of the "public spirit" of the days of Gustav II Adolf, i.e. the spirit that was supposed to have been buried shortly afterwards with Axel Oxenstierna and his generation.

As we have seen from Sven A. Nilsson's essay, however, new research has led to a reevaluation of the traditional view of the society of the great-power period; for example, the hoary myth that the freedom of the peasantry and the peasant economy were threatened by the transfer of lands to the nobility, a myth dating back to the quarrels between the Estates of the realm around 1650, has been laid to rest. New perspectives have shown different aspects of the period in a new light: it becomes difficult to imagine a worse time for the Swedish peasantry than the period of war during Gustav Adolf's reign, with its very heavy state taxation and frequent conscriptions. The figure of at least 50,000 men lost between 1621 and 1632 (out of Sweden and Finland's combined total of just over a million inhabitants) is another indication of the severe depletion of the country's population during these extremely hard years. The traditional preoccupation with the rule of the aristocracy thus proves a cul-de-sac, whereas the military-state perspective has turned out much more rewarding as a key to an understanding of the society of the seventeenth century and the changes that took place then.

The extensive transfer of landed estates was therefore a consequence of the need of the military state to reward and pay its warriors and its creditors, while at the same time it bound the nobility to the state. This belatedly put a great deal of land in the hands of the Swedish nobility, which constituted less than 0.5% of the total population, and especially in the hands of the higher nobility, i.e. the aristocracy, who could also count on the potentially most lucrative posts in the state administration. The nobility thus came to possess very large resources until the "feudal era" was superseded roughly half a century later by the society of the reduction and the allotment system with its different method of remuneration, a system that was more reliable and did not entail the personal sacrifice required by the previous one.

It is here that the aristocratic lifestyle comes into the picture, not the least important aspect being the prodigality with resources, which also deserves consideration from a new angle, that of seventeenth-century Sweden's need for social, economic and cultural development. In simple terms, the problem was not the old-fashioned nature of peasant agriculture so much as the fact that there was very little economic activity *other* than agriculture, i.e. little commerce, trade and industry. This was also how the problem was quickly seen by the Swedish government, which was at the same time concerned at Sweden's unimpressive status as a civilized nation. In the shadow of the all-pervading problems of the war, a reform programme, ambitious even if not immediately successful, was initiated with the object of modernizing the country. With this, great demands were made of the nobility by the regency council and by Axel Oxenstierna, who was the driving force behind the programme and who even saw a beneficial connection between the extravagance of the new aristocratic culture and the economic advance of the country.

An Age of Ambition

In March 1638 the *Kalmar Nyckel* and the *Fågel Grip*, two small ships that had set sail from Sweden the previous autumn, reached the Bay of Delaware on the east coast of North America. The expedition was led by the experienced German-Dutchman Peter Minuit – better known as the founder of New Amsterdam on Manhattan – who immediately began to establish the colony of New Sweden as instructed by Axel Oxenstierna. The first land was purchased from the Lenape Indians, Fort Christina began to rise on the site of present-day Wilmington, and fur trading with the Indians known to the Swedes as the Minquas began. Backing these enterprises was a new trading company, the New Sweden Company, with both Dutch and Swedish interests, the latter representing the Swedish government. Tobacco, in which the company was also to trade, was obtained on this occasion from St. Kitts (St. Christopher) in the West Indies on the return journey to Sweden.

When this happened, a very important *riksdag* had just closed in Sweden. Chancellor Axel Oxenstierna, whom we know from Sven A. Nilssson's essay as the leading organizer of the country's public administration and the man behind the Instrument of Government of 1634, had returned from Germany in the summer of 1636, but not until the autumn of the following year was it decided to call the Estates to a general *riksdag*. The delay testifies to the government's nervousness lest the Estates, once they got together, should seize the opportunity to demand relief from taxation, when the predicament of the country, both internal and external, demanded continued sacrifice. And indeed it was possible to accomplish a certain amount without the Estates' participation, such as the founding of the Board of Mines in 1637 and the planning of a Board of Commerce, both of which are indicative of the intensified efforts of those in power to develop the economy. But the need to raise more soldiers, combined with the parlous state of the exchequer, finally made the summoning of the *riksdag* inevitable.

The demands facing the Estates were therefore first and foremost for manpower and funds for the war currently in progress, which was a familiar situation during the difficult initial period of the Age of Greatness, as was the call for the nobility to renounce its tax privileges. The time also appeared ripe to try to deal with a number of recurring questions concerning the nation's internal finances. These included the problems of misappropriation of the little toll (the local market tolls) and of differences in weights and measures in different parts of the country, and also the threat posed to the forests by new settlement and by burning, and to the Crown parks by illegal felling and hunting. Another matter of business was the need to find ways of ensuring the settling of debts incurred by private individuals, a question that primarily affected the burghers and the nobility.

Cultural affairs were also discussed, but here the government addressed itself only to the Estate of the nobility, which was enjoined to provide for the training of its younger generation in noble arts and exercises and to be responsible for financing the building of the Palace of the Nobility. These questions, too, were not new ones. The building of a Palace of Nobility had been approved in 1625 and those nobles who had volunteered to contribute to its financing had already been asked at the *riksdagar* of the 1620s to pay up so that the work could start. At the same time the Estate had been urged to send its offspring to the planned college for the sons of the nobility, for which a Dutch engineer had already been appointed by 1628. (As Arne Losman has pointed out, a mastery of the science of fortifications engineering was among the accomplishments expected of a man of the world or *gentilhomme*.) Despite this, nothing had happened, which led Oxenstierna immediately on returning to Sweden to call attention to the need for a fencing school, a riding school and a dancing school, and also to the importance of arranging the financing of the Palace of the Nobility. The outcome of deliberations at the *riksdag* of 1638 on the first of these questions was that the nobility asked to be allowed to use the teachers of languages, dancing and riding who had in any case to be maintained at the royal court. As far as the building of the Palace of the Nobility was concerned, a reluctant and divided nobility was prevailed upon – by the vigorous efforts of the chancellor – to agree to a personal contribution far in excess of what they considered they could afford. On the other hand, no sumptuary ordinance, such as the Estate of the nobility had called for some years previously and now called for again, was issued. Nevertheless, the government agreed that the ostentatious extravagance accompanying weddings and funerals was causing difficulty to the nobility – an extravagance in which the poorly off felt obliged to indulge "like the rich" in order not to be "disdained and despised".

At about this time, at Stockholm Castle, a performance of the French ballet *des Plaisirs de la Vie des Enfants sans Soucy* took place for the entertainment of the young Queen Christina, still only eleven years old; this is the first recorded occasion of a ballet's being danced in Sweden. It was produced by the French dancing and ballet master Antoine de Beaulieu, who had been recruited to Sweden the previous year, and the dancers were the young gentlemen of the court, i.e. representatives of the "second generation" of the aristocracy. Among them could have been observed the fifteen-year-old Magnus Gabriel De la Gardie and also Lorentz von der Linde, nearly ten years his senior and strictly speaking not a member of the aristocracy at all, although a future baron, councillor of the realm and field marshal. His father, who had recently died, was the prominent merchant Eric Larsson von der Linde, himself the son of an immigrant Dutch merchant. Eric Larsson had been involved in Holland in the extensive credit-raising operations, based on the security of Swedish copper, that were essential to Swedish participation in the war at this time, and he had himself advanced large sums to the Crown. He had been ennobled for these services in 1631 and part of his loans had been repaid in landed property. There were three things that this man was said never to be prepared to divulge: how much money he had put into his new house in Stockholm, what he had lost in damage sustained at sea and what he had spent on his son Lorentz! An investment that had clearly paid dividends.

These three seemingly very disparate events – the founding of a Swedish colony in America, the eventful *riksdag* of 1638 and the Swedish première of French courtly ballet – have more in common than their approximately simultaneous occurrence, which is in fact no coincidence. They not only give an indication of the intention of the government to reform Sweden, an intention expressed more forcefully after the chancellor's return home. On closer inspection the events also illustrate the difficulties that needed to be overcome. A dire warning came in the serious disturbances that at once broke out among the peasantry in response to the new war burdens and the more efficient collection of tolls. Some projects failed very quickly, such as the New Sweden venture, to which I shall return, while others would take decades to carry out, such as the building of the Palace of the Nobility, which was not finally completed until the 1670s. Only the court ballet, which came to play an important part in courtly festivities and thus in the panegyric art of which Allan Ellenius has written, was an immediate success. In other words, the culture of the aristocracy could be modernized more quickly than the nation's economy.

The Swedes were not alone in seeking to copy foreign models; similar ambitions were a feature of the building of all the new nation-states. In the cultural sphere it was first Italy and later France that set the tone, while in the economic sphere it was first Holland, then England. The distinctive aspects of the Swedish situation were perhaps that everything had to be done at once and that the aristocracy was to lead the way in the work of modernization, which had however begun under the strong direction of Gustav II Adolf or in some cases even earlier.

The improvement of mining and the development of the towns, for instance, had been on Gustav Adolf's programme, which envisaged the expansion of domestic industry for the purpose. The regency pursued the same policy, while at the same time the development of towns, manufactories, trade and shipping – "following the example of others" – gradually came to be regarded as a means of bringing money into the country with the aid of a favourable balance of trade. This principle was clearly exemplified at an early date by the proposal to establish a Board of Commerce in 1637, and Oxenstierna has been described as one of the foremost introducers of mercantilism in Sweden. But customs policy was still shaped by the fiscal needs of the military state (protectionism belongs to a later era), and the development of shipping also had as an objective the strengthening of the navy. By granting special privileges for certain kinds of manufacture or trade it would be possible to attract foreigners with large capital resources to Sweden, and they would not infrequently loan money to the state. The most celebrated of them all arrived while Gustav Adolf was still on the throne. This was Louis De Geer, who came to be known as the father of Swedish industry. In addition specialist skilled labour was also to be imported and there is mention at one point of recruiting a company of flax weavers. But the object had to be to make the country independent of foreigners by training Swedes. Such, at any rate, was the attitude taken by Carl Bonde, councillor of the realm and president of the Board of Mines, when in 1640 he proudly announced that Swedish carpenters could now make lock gates of wood that were as good as those made of stone by imported Dutch lock builders.

The plea for a higher level of cultivation reflected even more clearly the need for self-assertion. When Oxenstierna inspected Uppsala University in 1637, for example, it was decided that botanical gardens should be laid out and an anatomical theatre built, both of which projects, as we have seen, were realized only in the time of Olof Rudbeck. The anatomical theatre was to be provided with instruments, skeletons and rarities that would enable both Swedes and foreigners to observe things in Sweden that had hitherto been on view only overseas. The need for self-assertion is most plainly expressed in the plans of the regency council for the nobility, which was to be the backbone of the new state.

The reign of Gustav II Adolf was stated at the *riksdag* of 1638 to have marked the beginning of a new period in the history of the nobility, which had been oppressed and scorned abroad and had been unworthy of comparison with the nobility of other nations. The Palace of the Nobility was to be a visible symbol of the nobility's new status, while at the same time the nobles, before being sent on government service, were to have to possess all kinds of accomplishments, which ought first to be practised at home, before being perfected in the course of study abroad. If we consider, for example, the relatively impecunious Carl Bonde, we see how strongly – and early – these ambitions were felt. In 1632 he is taking pleasure in his sons' command (at the ages of twelve and ten) of French; in 1634 he is lamenting the fact that at the University of Uppsala they receive neither instruction in "mores" nor training in noble exercises and in 1638 we find the sons being sent with their tutor to England, from there to continue to Holland and France. Financial assistance was given initially by Axel Oxenstierna and his banker, Peter Spiring, originally a Dutchman, now a Swede.

Two very interesting discussions linking the financial and the cultural spheres took place in the council in the spring of 1641. In the first case the point at issue was how to stop the outflow of Swedish coin and capital. Oxenstierna then rejected the sumptuary law, proposed, surprisingly, by the burgomaster of Stockholm, giving three reasons for its rejection: (1) the difficulty of getting people to observe such a law, (2) the fact that steps were just being taken to "civilize the nation" and (3) the importance of attracting trade and commerce to the country. In the second case the discussion was complicated by the difficulty of resolving the question of the disposal of landed estates in order to meet the state's critical financial problems, a subject that was especially delicate during the queen's minority. Discussion then moved on to how Sweden could best emulate other countries' cultural standards in general. It was decided that this would be best done firstly by founding towns and promoting trade and manufacturing industry,

which could be expected to yield large profits from town tolls and excise duties (implying the much-needed revenues in cash rather than in kind, it might have been added), and secondly by relying on the nobility to build up the country.

Oxenstierna's well-known programme for the state finances is presented here as plainly as anyone could wish, as is the much less noticed call for cultural renewal and transformation that accompanies it. The broad signification of "culture" should be noted, as should the strong expectation that the nobility will participate in the social transformation. Last but not least, Oxenstierna's realization of the importance of a real domestic demand in successfully bringing about the required changes ought to be observed.

There might therefore be a desirable side to the spendthrift lifestyle of the social elite, a suggestion to which I shall return. But I must first refer to the possible connection between the New Sweden venture and the contemporary process of nation-building with its social background. There is reason to consider these matters in some detail, although without going into the full history of the enterprise.

The Case of New Sweden

New Sweden was to enjoy an existence of only seventeen years. Consequently, it never became the gleaming jewel in the Swedish crown which the Dutchman Willem Usselinx had predicted in the early 1630s that a Swedish colony in America could become and into which even the last governor, Johan Rising, believed New Sweden could still develop, if only supplies and colonists were sent without delay from the mother country. Rising's opinion may be read in an optimistic report written in July 1654, soon after his arrival. But by September 1655 Rising was compelled to cede the colony to Peter Stuyvesant, the energetic governor of New Netherland, who was in turn forced, nine years later, to capitulate to the English.

With the exception of Rising, a few officers and soldiers and a small number of other colonists, most of the Swedes chose to remain in America. Many of them had just arrived with the tenth expedition from their homeland, which had given a much needed boost to the settlers' numbers. Previously the population of the colony had not only been small but also included remarkably few farmers, or freemen as they were known, which did not augur particularly well for the prospects of a colonial enterprise. At the time of the Dutch capture there were roughly 400 Swedes in New Sweden, in about 130 households, together with a couple of hundred other colonists of other nationalities who had been allowed to settle there. The total number of Swedish voyagers to America in the mid-seventeenth century was probably at least twice as many, however, but not all of them reached New Sweden, and some left the colony again to return home or settle elsewhere. Moreover there were a number who did not arrive until the Swedish era had already come to an end. Many were Finns who had come either from Sweden, some forest areas of which had quite a sizable Finnish population, or from Finland itself. There were also people of foreign origin, as in most Swedish contexts at this period. In any event, the Swedes were never numerous, particularly by comparison with the total number of Europeans in the coastal colonies, from Virginia in the south to New England in the north, which was probably around 100,000 in the 1660s.

To many people in the tracts where the colony's institutions and the colonists' settlements once stood, in the states of Delaware, Pennsylvania, New Jersey and Maryland, a lively interest in New Sweden is taken as a matter of course; people speak of the contribution of the New Sweden Swedes to American civilization and of "the Swedish heritage", which can be touched on only briefly here. The Swedes and their descendants, estimated in the second decade of the eighteenth century to number about 1,500 persons, existed as a distinct ethnic group for over a century. One reason for this was that for a long time pastors were sent over by the mother country to minister to the Swedish Lutheran congregations in the area, to which the survival of six old chur-

The Swedish parish registration system was transferred to the Swedish congregations of North America.

Register of members of the congregation of Christine parish, made by the local pastor (Rev. Anders Borell) November 8, 1764.

William Vaneman, speaks Swedish perfectly, reads the Bible in both Swedish and English, knows the catechism well, understands the sermon well, attends Communion, 53 years old, merchant, farmer ... daughter Johanna, goes to school.

ches today bears witness. Of these, the Holy Trinity Church in Wilmington, consecrated in 1699, is the oldest church in America still standing on its original site and in use for services, while the Gloria Dei Church (now the Old Swedes' Church) in Philadelphia is the oldest church in Pennsylvania. Another Swedish influence is to be found in the field of housebuilding, where the Swedes' choice of timber as their building material, together with their special corner-timber technique, gave rise to the log cabin, which seems quickly to have become standard in all settlement of the wooded regions of North America. It has also been said that to some extent the later Colonial style of the American settler had its roots in the Swedes' log cabin.

The leading chronicler of the New Sweden enterprise is the Swedish-American Amandus Johnson, whose *The Swedish Settlements on the Delaware 1638–1664* was published in 1911, but as was mentioned by way of introduction, there is a copious literature on New Sweden. As colonists Swedes have generally earned good ratings, where as Sweden as a colonizing power has been portrayed in a less favourable light. The reason usually given for the initiation of the New Sweden venture is Oxenstierna's wish to find new markets for Swedish copper or the need for new sources of income after the loss of revenue from licences to trade through the Prussian ports in 1635. The failure of the project has in turn been attributed to the inadequate support it received from the mother country as a result of the government's preoccupation with war and the alleged indifference of Queen Christina to affairs of state. The wreck of the *Kattan* in 1649, with the loss of the ninth expedition from Sweden and some seventy would-be colonists, has also been seen as very important, as have certain mistakes said to have been made by Governor Rising in the face of the threat from the Dutch. In addition it has recently been argued that the project was in any case doomed to failure as Peter Minuit applied to the founding of New Sweden the same set of assumptions as to New Amsterdam twelve years earlier and did not take into account Sweden's insufficiency of deep-sea tonnage.

It has to be agreed that the New Sweden enterprise had no hope of success, especially as both the Dutch and the English claimed the area at the mouth of the Delaware. And it is very true that the lack of vessels and, more particularly, of experienced seamen, was a problem. But the interesting thing about the transport question is that this was in fact one of the main reasons for the Swedish interest in the enterprise. Time after time when New Sweden was discussed in council, a reason given for the government's involvement – in addition to the primary motive of an increase in trade – was that the nation would gain practice in navigation. This is how it was put in 1642, for example, when the reconstitution of the company was under consideration, and when shipping in the Atlantic was being discussed in 1646 Oxenstierna gave as reasons for the participation of the Crown's ships in trade with Portugal and Virginia "not profit alone" but also the fact that the people were "being trained" in navigation. On another occasion, Oxenstierna said that with the aid of seafarers it would be possible to build up not only the fleet but also cities, thus augmenting the nation's income; here he was quoting Admiral Clas Fleming, who together with Oxenstierna was the venture's leading Swedish initiator. Trading companies were also considered to stimulate domestic shipbuilding, which was important if the expenditure on chartering and shipping charges was to remain in the country. The presence of oak forests in the colony and the possibility of building ships there, about which careful enquiries had been made, contributed to the decision in 1652 to make a renewed commitment to New Sweden, whereupon the direction of the company was entrusted to the Board of Commerce that had now come into being.

The New Sweden enterprise was thus a part of the reform programme that was currently under way, i.e. of that section of it which was designed to develop trade and shipping and which required the assistance of foreign capital and mercantilist knowhow. It is significant that the queen's first question to Louis De Geer, who had already settled in Sweden, when his charter for a company to trade in Africa, Asia and America was being discussed in 1649, was whether foreigners, too, would be offered the chance to become part-owners, to which De Geer answered affirmatively, while her second was whether he intended to build ships.

That the New Sweden enterprise has to be seen in this context is confirmed by its prelude, which included the persistent wooing of the Swedish government by a group of Dutch entrepreneurs. A couple of these Dutchmen had been involved in the Dutch West India Company but, having become dissatisfied there, were offering their services to others. The first was the aforementioned Willem Usselinx, the founder of the Dutch West India Company, who was granted the Southern Company licence by Gustav II Adolf in the 1620s. The only mention that need be made of this decidedly unsuccessful company here is that large profits were predicted when the nobility was exhorted to subscribe to shares at the *riksdag* of 1627 and that the English and Dutch East and West India companies were pointed to as models. The last in the series of Dutchmen to lay out his stall was Minuit, who had been director-general of the Dutch West India Company and governor of New Netherland but lost his position after a dispute with his employers. Minuit joined his compatriots Samuel Blommaert and Peter Spiring, both active in Holland on Sweden's behalf, who were trying to interest the Swedish government in plans for a company trading in Africa, particularly the Guinea Coast. The birth of the New Sweden company, with five Swedish and six Dutch stockholders, appears to have been the result of Spiring's efforts – he was government adviser on customs matters and had become a Swedish nobleman in 1636. But it was undoubtedly Minuit's experience that led to the decision to make America and the Delaware the focus of the company's trading activities and to combine the company with a colonization project, and it was on the lines of his plan, as presented to Oxenstierna, that the venture was launched.

In these circumstances it must obviously have been a blow to the Swedes when the Dutch participants wanted to withdraw as soon as the first expedition arrived back home. The setback was surely all the more severe in view of the fact that Oxenstierna strongly favoured a system that left trading to private enterprise and – unlike Gustav Adolf – was no friend of state-controlled trading companies. The reason for the Dutch wish to back out was probably that they did not want to or did not dare challenge the Dutch West India Company, in which they were also stockholders, particularly as the new company seemed to offer little hope of profit. Moreover Minuit had disappeared, in mysterious circumstances, on the journey home.

The founding of New Sweden was not therefore, as has sometimes been maintained, inspired by a dream of extending the Swedish empire to the New World. The enterprise was the result of an alliance between Dutchmen with short-term profit motives and representatives of the Swedish government who wanted to strengthen and consolidate the existing Swedish empire. The Swedish participants were, in addition to Oxenstierna and Fleming, two close relatives of Oxenstierna who were both members of the government, and Peter Spiring, ennobled as Silfvercrona. To the first four of these, partnership was not a demonstration of entrepreneurial spirit but a contribution comparable to the many "voluntary" efforts which had been made by the aristocracy in various contexts (including trading companies), and which councillors of the realm, in particular, were expected to make by way of a good example. The remarkable thing on this occasion is that so few contributed. "If all would contribute a few hundred *daler*, so that the country can be colonized..." records a laconic minute of the meeting of the council in March 1639, when New Sweden was being discussed. And when the company was to be reorganized as a fully Swedish concern, a reason given for the Crown's entry as a partner was that private individuals lacked the capacity to operate the company on their own, which has been interpreted in the historiography of New Sweden as meaning that they lacked the capital. What has been overlooked is that the time was extremely poorly chosen for a venture of the kind planned by Minuit.

I am referring here to the condition of Sweden in the 1630s and first and foremost of its scanty population, which has led one historian to describe the country as "a land of soldiers' widows". The peasantry was in a state of unrest and large numbers of soldiers were deserting; nobles were complaining of the difficulty of finding labour and that their farmsteads were lying desolate, and in a debate on the problems of the towns by the council in 1636 it was agreed that without a larger population any attempt to build large cities in Sweden would be in vain. But Sweden was a thinly populated country even in normal times: as Per Brahe put it in 1645, Sweden had "few people and much land", whereas abroad there were "many people and little land". The time was hardly right for a colonization project.

When the company was reorganized in 1642, no attempt seems to have been made to increase the number of private stockholders. However the company received an infusion of capital from the practically dissolved South Ship Company and the Crown became a partner, confirming the character of the company as a state concern. That the intention was that "colonists in large numbers were to be sent over for the development of the country" has been assumed by Amandus Johnson and by other writers; they have also drawn the conclusion that it was the difficulty of obtaining sufficient willing emigrants in the early stages that made it necessary to resort to using New Sweden as a transportation colony for Finns from the mining areas of central Sweden – where their slash-and-burn methods of agriculture were regarded as a menace to the forests – and also for criminals of various kinds.

The fact is that nothing can be said with any degree of certainty about the intended number of colonists, but it is worth noting that it was the governors of certain counties in central Sweden, where tax-privileged land was virtually non-existent, who were asked to recruit colonists. As conscription did not normally take place in these areas either, this also meant that disruption of the armed forces was kept to a minimum. Nevertheless it was impossible wholly to avoid a conflict of interest between the need for colonists and domestic considerations, as may have been experienced by the county governor who was ordered to build cities in his province and fill them with people, or by Carl Bonde, who used Finnish labour in the ironworks and on canal-building. When in 1649 the queen was surprised to find that three hundred Finns wished to sail to New Sweden, as she thought there was surely enough land for settlement in Sweden, she was not revealing a lack of interest in affairs of state but expressing her view that domestic needs should be given priority, just as when a few months later she declared that the people who had been taken over to the colony were needed at home.

The government's dilemma – whether to colonize New Sweden or to attend to needs that had been declared to have higher priority – is evident from the use of the settlement as a transportation colony. While it might be desirable to induce Finns to emigrate rather than burning the forests, it would also be a good thing if they could be persuaded to settle permanently in vacant homesteads. It should also be noted that the government showed itself well aware of the particular complications of the early stages of the colonization project. This is evident from what was said in 1639 when a county governor was ordered to pardon all married soldiers who were for any reason under sentence of death, provided that they departed for New Sweden with their families. It was pointed out that the matter had to be handled with a very sure touch, because even though it was important for sailing to New Sweden to continue and the colony to be populated with Swedes, it was even more urgent for Swedish subjects to be treated in such a manner as to discourage insurrection. The serious disturbances of 1638 were fresh in mind.

In the years that followed, banishment to New Sweden was frequently proposed in connection with various felonies, but this method cannot actually have produced many colonists. Transportation was not a new form of punishment, however, which gives us cause to note an important difference between New Sweden and other colonized areas. In former times both rebellious peasants and people guilty of damaging oak forest or of illegal hunting had been banished to Ingria, which had been Swedish since 1617; the aristocracy had received estates there and good care had been taken to populate them. But the aristocracy had no landed estates in New Sweden, and one of Sweden's largest landowners was highly indignant when Oxenstierna suggested that she should pay the cost of crossing to New Sweden for a thieving servant. Moreover the colony lay a long way from the centre of power and it is significant that no member of the aristocracy ever visited it, although several of the untitled nobility served there. A condemned and reprieved officer, Matthias Franke, who had in 1645 to be provided with a post – but not a "superior" post – was, however, the type of person that the council could contemplate sending to New Sweden.

Sweden's performance as a colonizer in the New World has to be judged in the light of the country's circumstances. Bearing in mind the process of nation-building that was taking place and what the Swedes hoped to accomplish from the New Sweden enterprise, it is easy to see that a whole-hearted and successful commitment to colonization was hardly to be expected from the Swedish government at this time and that a trading station would have been more appropriate than a colony. Once the colony was in existence, however, there was generally a wish to preserve it – with the isolated exception of one occasion in 1649 when the queen and certain councillors questioned the value of both the company and the colony. But an increased availability of willing colonists, together with the establishment of the Board of Commerce, was undoubtedly one of the factors behind the renewed decision in 1652 to invest further resources in the venture. There is a kind of logic in the fact that it was the secretary of the Board of Commerce, Johan Rising, who was to be the colony's last governor. Rising was also an economic theorist and a writer of mercantilist views and his optimistic plans for the colony, including the founding of cities, manufactories and extensive new plantations, meant that the re-

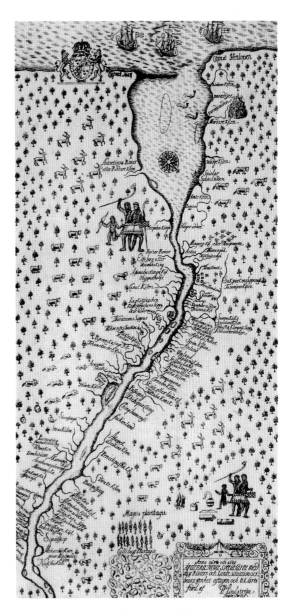

Per Lindeström's map of the Colony of New Sweden.
Royal Swedish Military Record Office.
Photo: Royal Swedish Military Record Office.

shaping of commerce on Dutch lines that was proposed in Sweden was to be extended to the colony. That the plans were unrealistic hardly needs stating. On the other hand it may be worthy of note that Rising not only calls for craftsmen, essential supplies and colonists to be sent over from the mother country but also *Dutch* colonists, which gives food for thought. Slash-and-burn peasants were probably all right for breaking new soil, but they were not the right kind of worker for the commercial society that Rising was planning or for the growing of tobacco, or the planting of mulberry trees for silkworm farms, or for sheep-farming, all of which had been mentioned back in 1642 as urgent tasks for the colony.

The growing of tobacco in the colony would eliminate the need for the company to buy its tobacco from English and Dutch merchants in the area. The profits would go to the company, consistent with the mercantilist principle of obtaining the goods one needed from a primary source. As far as the company's trade is concerned, all that need be stated here is that most of the tobacco brought to Sweden in the company's ships was bought from merchants in America and Europe, not cultivated in the colony, and that the greater part of the merchandise needed for trade with the Indians, such as cloth, axes, adzes, knives, copper kettles etc. had been purchased in Holland, not produced in Sweden. In other words, it was not only as a colonization project that New Sweden came at the wrong time. Finally there proved to be little demand in Sweden for the pelts (mostly beaver skins) that were a classic luxury article in other countries. For that reason Fleming wondered in 1642 whether the furs ought to be sent for sale in Holland, but Spiring did not agree and took the view that the merchants ought rather to come to Sweden – a logical attitude if the primary consideration was the interest of the Crown in form of increased customs revenues.

An Overlooked Boom

For foreign merchants to come to Sweden (and preferably to settle there), their wares naturally had to be in demand. A domestic demand for goods and services was also essential if the cities that had been laid out and the manufactories that were planned were to have a chance of prospering. But a characteristic of Swedish society was of course the limited size of the market (i.e. of demand) and the predominance of the barter economy. This had to be changed before any investment could be more than a futile gesture. We shall now look at how the consumption patterns of the international elite lifestyle came to Sweden and how the new demand for luxuries helped in various ways to overcome the problem of the smallness of the market.

The need for a sumptuary ordinance to curb the extravagance of the nobility, which was in the air in 1638, suggests that something new was happening. The background was a process that had begun much earlier, at the time when Sweden embarked on an expansionist policy in the 1560s. Both Erik XIV and Johan III behaved like Renaissance princes, as may be seen from the palaces they built. The assimilation of the aristocracy in the courtly culture of Europe, on the other hand, was more problematical. There were several highly educated humanists and bibliophiles, and there was contact with the Italian Renaissance, but by European standards the Swedish aristocracy was impoverished. Moreover it was long restrained by monarchic power, as demonstrated by the execution of several of its leaders in 1600. Not until the reign of Gustav II Adolf did things change. The building of magnificent private mansions that was seen in the late Renaissance in Denmark, in England and on the Continent thus has no counterpart in Sweden. The tardiness of developments in Sweden is also shown by the fact that noble sumptuary legislation was passed in Denmark in the 1570s, but not in Sweden until 1644. When the Swedish aristocracy really began to increase its consumption of luxuries, the peak had almost been reached in other countries.

The dramatic increase in consumption by the aristocracy in other countries has been seen as arising from the need of the new nation states for a representative public face and from the existence of a princely-aristocratic pattern of consumption, for which the royal courts set the standard. In Sweden, too, the monarchy led the way and the luxurious living of seventeenth-century Sweden started as a peaceful branch of great-power politics. The competition within the courtly society of absolutism, which resulted abroad in a battle in which consumption was a weapon, has, however, no equivalent in Sweden, where absolutism came later. On the other hand, local Swedish conditions did nothing to reduce competition, rather the reverse. In Sweden as abroad, what was important was conspicuous consumption, designed to serve as a status symbol (it should be noted that the concept tells us nothing about the quality of the luxuries consumed). Most of the main areas of consumption spotlighted by Lawrence Stone with reference to the English aristocracy were also favoured in Sweden, namely the building of houses and their use for entertainment involving armies of servants and outrageously lavish festivities, costume, coaches (the Rolls-Royces of the day) and expensive funerals. The only exception was gambling, the great age of which comes later in Sweden.

If this kind of consumption was late in starting in Sweden, it made up for it by quickly reaching a very impressive level, which may be explained by a combination of the assertiveness of a new great power and domestic rivalry for influence, favour and social prestige. By the 1630s competition was in full swing, Treasurer of the Realm Gabriel Bengtsson Oxenstierna having just built himself a country house said to be "the envy of the city" by Ogier, who at the same time praises the residences of Eric Larsson von der Linde, both in the capital and in the country. A few years later Axel Oxenstierna's Tidö was complete, work on it having begun in the 1620s, and the French architect Simon De la Vallée was engaged as architect to the aristocracy and the royal family.

The upswing of the 1630s is naturally linked to the fact that after the death of the king responsibility for the country's cultural image fell on the regency council and the aristocracy, to whom public and private spheres lar-

gely coincided. But an additional factor was the leading role that the nobility was expected to take in the building of the nation, a role that required training in noble arts and a courtly lifestyle. "In the past we have always kept our solemnities to ourselves," objected a member of the council (not altogether accurately), who feared that the shoddiness of the great power facade would be revealed if emissaries from abroad were invited to the king's funeral. And when a few years later Jacob De la Gardie and his wife Ebba Brahe were expecting foreign visitors at Jakobsdal, the interior of the new country house was spruced up with the aid of furniture from their home in Stockholm – in order to demonstrate "that we live properly in this country, too". Rivalry for status within the aristocracy further raised the level of consumption, as did the fact that businessmen and officials who had not yet been, or only recently been, ennobled indulged equally frenetically in conspicuous consumption. von der Linde has already been mentioned, while Louis De Geer built the first Palladian mansion in Stockholm during the years 1646–1650, having on the same site already erected one in German-Dutch Renaissance style that he now intended to demolish. Before long the point had been reached where an older Swedish aristocrat, Jacob De la Gardie, could have a staff of servants equal to that of the English aristocracy at the height of that country's excesses (his son Magnus Gabriel then doubled the number). Nor did the intended public relations effect fail to materialize: as early as 1649 a Spanish envoy was reporting that consumption of luxuries was greater in Sweden, in relation to resources, than in any other country.

In the 1650s the trend accelerated. The reason was keener competition, in conjunction with a change in taste and style that took place at that time, if not earlier, for it should be noted that the Gallic predilections of the nobility were already evident in the 1630s, when Axel Oxenstierna was busy on a magnificent residence in the French style on his own account, and many had, like Carl Gustav Wrangel, already visited Paris. There are many testimonies to the fiercer rivalry that followed the

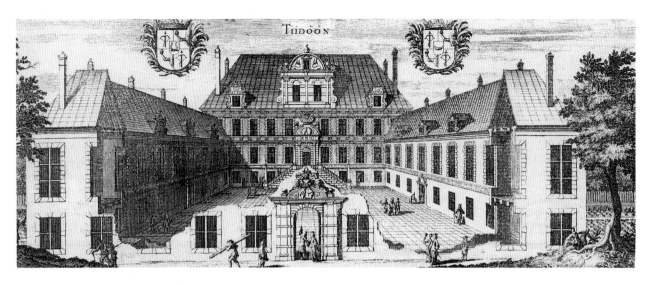

Axel Oxenstierna's Tidö in the province of Västmanland.
From Suecia Antiqua.

conclusion of peace, such as that of the fortifications officer Erik Dahlbergh (artist and architect and still a commoner although a future count), who feared that his promotion would be delayed by the numerous sons of magnates in his way. He therefore accepted the offer of service as tutor and travelling companion to the newly created barons Cronstierna, thus joining the ranks of young men of limited means who found such a route to foreign study. It was also at this stage that the oft-mentioned new generation took over. In the course of a few years in the 1650s several older magnates died and the resulting intensification of rivalry may be clearly seen in the fantastic splendour of many of the funerals, at which fine processions also offered both a pretext and a stage for further struggles for precedence. To this has to be added the effect of two coronations in four years, those of Christina in 1650 and Karl X Gustav in 1654, producing mounting opulence in both dress and coaches.

While costs were rocketing, the previous steady growth in the nobility's income stopped, as donation of lands came to a halt, a partial reduction (repossession of lands by the Crown) was ordered and personal taxation was introduced. The increased luxury expenditure had, in other words, to be met from a reduced income. Moreover the death of Karl X Gustav in 1660 restored to the aristocracy a kind of ultimate cultural responsibility, even though there was at this time a dazzling competitor in the shape of the dowager queen, Hedvig Eleonora, particularly when it came to building projects. The characteristic tendency throughout the remaining period until the upheavals of the 1680s was a quantitative and qualitative increase in luxurious living – nothing else was possible. Far too many had been inspired with the same spirit as Treasurer of the Realm Gustav Bonde, known as an opponent of De la Gardie and an advocate of thrift in the regency of Karl XI, but himself a great builder. Stockholm's first private mansion in the Parisian style, completed in the 1660s, was his achievement. Bonde's will stipulated that the new mansion had to remain in the family in perpetuity, as he

Ceremonial coach of Karl XI.
The Royal Armoury.
Photo: Göran Schmidt.

*Erik Dahlberg's design proposals for Gustav Bonde's mansion in
Stockholm. Royal Swedish Library.
Photo: Royal Swedish Library.*

had built it more for the glory of the family than for his
own comfort. The aim of conspicuous consumption
can scarcely be better formulated.

The new pattern of consumption was not therefore
something to be adopted only according to one's
means. It was *de rigueur* in all the leading circles of
society, to which more and more people considered
themselves to belong, and this accounts for its spread. It
was also copied by ambitious groups outside the nobility. As far as dress is concerned, Katharina Wallen-
stedt, herself the wife of a civil servant of the untitled
nobility in the Stockholm of the 1670s, fretted over the
fact that people of her acquaintance adopted a finer style
of dress even before they received their letter of
ennoblement. And just as the aristocracy kept abreast of
Paris fashion, so the provincial nobility kept itself informed of the fashions of the capital. It may be added
that the obsession with status was less furious in the
country than in Stockholm, where there were more
people to indulge in it. But according to Katharina Wal-
lenstedt, the capital was the place to be: although life
there was much more expensive, it was nearer to the
seats of power. The proud housebuilding bears witness
to the ambitions of the merchant class, particularly in
Stockholm, and in the 1660s sumptuary ordinances
were extended to the clergy and the burghers, who were
urged not to dress above their station and to refrain from
extravagance at feasts and funerals. As usual in such cases, the prohibitions had no effect.

Neither commission of inquiry, reduction and absolutism nor the wars of Karl XII put an end to the consumption of luxuries, although it assumes a different

Maria Sophia De la Gardie, 1643. Maltesholm.
Photo: Swedish Portrait Archives.

Burgher's wife Barbro Blanck, 1654. Hälsingland Museum,
Hudiksvall.
Photo: Solveig Berglund.

character in the final phase of the great-power period. What may at first seem to be a consequence of a radical deterioration in personal finances or of the monarch's disapproval of ostentatious consumption – as has been mentioned in connection with Karl XI – may also be attributable rather to new artistic impulses and international changes of fashion or even be an expression of a certain satiation. The importance of the monarch's attitude is reduced by the fact that many of the men of the new autocracy were at home with the elite lifestyle as a result of earlier service with the titled nobility or the royal family. Several had also had time to earn a reputation for luxurious living well before absolutism, and in Karl XII Sweden once more had a monarch with a liking for splendour and display, at least until war gave him other things to think about. At the king's prompting and with Nicodemus Tessin the Younger as the chief organizer there were several years of hectic entertainment, with theatricals, masquerades, balls and pageants, very much in the spirit of the court of France.

In the field of building, the monarchy once again took over the initiative, even in the reign of Karl XI, whom Tessin hade made aware of the opportunities for princely glorification afforded by the Baroque. The fantastic building boom created by the projects of the nobility, which had lasted ever since the 1630s, thus died out in the 1680s. Really large private projects, such as Tessin's personal mansion, in very close proximity to the royal palace, are the exception at the end of the century. The newly rich and the newly ennobled, when looking for homes appropriate to their social status, were in many cases able to move into existing mansions and manor houses, purchased, acquired by marriage or leased. As work started on the building of the new palace, a price ceiling was imposed for bricks and a royal option declared on all lime and bricks produced in Sweden. In other cases it is the burghers who build in Stockholm in the eighteenth century, and the holders of civil and military allotments who build their dwellings elsewhere. At the same time a number of the old Stockholm residences, as if by design, become manufactories.

A decline in the building of private mansions necessarily implies that the level of ostentatious extravagance fell during the final period of the Age of Greatness. Against this, it seems that the demand for luxury goods became more widespread and that conspicuous consumption did not disappear. There were complaints that servants were too well dressed, and in the case of one of the nobility's finest status symbols – the coach – it was demanded early in the eighteenth century that only the nobility and the military command should have the right to use such vehicles, in order to maintain the difference between the Estates of the realm. Not only the nobility but also the *haute bourgeoisie* queued for the portrait painter Martin Mijtens, and among the buyers at the auction following the death of Maria Sophia De la Gardie in 1694 was not only the privy councillor Carl Piper but also the tapestry maker Gudmund Törnqvist, who bought an expensive mirror.

The tremendous increase in consumption among the seventeenth-century nobility had a devastating effect on the private finances of many of them. The building projects, which were the most expensive item of expenditure, generally cost twice as much as at first estimated, as well as tying up resources for a long time to come. When Field-Marshal Lennart Torstensson died in 1651 he left a number of uncompleted buildings, including a mansion in Stockholm that his son Anders was unable to move into until 1664. Similarly Gustav Bonde, who died in 1667, left the mansion that has already been mentioned unfinished and encumbered with enormous mortgages. Emerging worse off from inquiry into the administration of the regency and from the reduction, his widow was obliged to sell the mansion, although it was restored to the family when the son made a wealthy marriage.

The extravagance thus led inevitably to private debt that grew enormously and an equivalent to the deficit economy characteristic of the courtly society of absolutist France and of England a hundred years earlier was definitely not lacking in Sweden. By way of example we may consider Claes Tott, a councillor of the realm,

Tessin's mansion in Stockholm. Photo: Gösta Glase.

125

whose annual income from his landed estates and his offices totalled just over 23,000 silver *daler,* while his expenses were somewhere between 35,000 and 50,000 *daler.* The debts of the nobility led to legal actions and to changes of ownership of lands and farms, but the aristocracy in particular seems to have put off the day of liquidation. Many aristocrats therefore reached the 1680s and their upheavals with hopelessly undermined finances.

Although the circumstances have not been investigated with any great thoroughness, it is not difficult to see that parallel with this process there was a transfer of wealth in large and small portions to groups outside the nobility, who supplied the nobility and the royal family with goods, services and credit. The categories of the population that this involved were in part those who assisted the military state, but only in part. One person who made himself rich on the demand for luxury goods was Claude Roquette, a merchant of French origin who was ennobled as Hägerstierna and soon owned his house in Stockholm, another just outside the capital and estates elsewhere in the country. The shift of economic strength to certain parts of the bourgeoisie and to civil servants of the untitled nobility whose roots lay in this class, which we first see clearly towards the end of the century, must be the result of a process that had begun much earlier.

But luxury consumption not only required capital and credit, it also created employment and was labour-intensive, and to a large extent it demanded payment in ready money. This latter fact seems to have led to agreements between landowners and peasants, in those cases that have been studied, on permanent taxes payable in cash. Payment in cash instead of in kind transferred the onus of conversion to the taxpayers, resulting in a growth in the cash economy and in the incipient market integration of peasant agriculture. The rapidly rising demand for timber, stone and other building materials and for meat and dairy products for entertaining must also have helped to bring about a reorientation of production. There were cases of builders competing for boards and planks, and rises in the prices paid for the peasant's timber were noted. Whom this benefitted most, however – the peasants or the merchants – is uncertain.

The vigorous growth of the artisan class and the fact that a pattern of specialist trades now emerged that would survive until the nineteenth century were both directly and indirectly related with the new pattern of consumption. In the purely luxury crafts, moreover, it seems that not only material costs but also labour costs were considerable. This may be why so many goldsmiths were able to lend money to the nobility. A number of the artists and architects enjoyed brilliant careers in society. There was also a remarkable increase in the number of servants, which might include everything from butlers, tutors and private chaplains to washer-women. There were great differences in their remuneration, exaggerated by the generous gifts to certain occupational categories.

But it is the labour required for building that is most striking. In return for exemption from other taxation many peasants did far more days' work than before. This work was largely done on the new building projects while the landlord's home farm (at the castle or manor house) was barely kept ticking over in the absence of adequate labour. In addition, innumerable assorted labourers, female helpers and carriers, and soldiers, together with a large number of craftsmen of various kinds, were employed. In these dealings, too, wages were paid – at least partly – in cash, which, together with the demand for transport of building materials, greatly increased the peasant's opportunity for subsidiary income. Finally, the unprecedently lavish funeral ceremonies gave ample scope for extra earnings for musicians, clergy, schoolboys, soldiers and many others, and there were loud complaints when the funeral processions were abolished at the end of the century.

Seen from this perspective, and bearing in mind the specific need of seventeenth-century Swedish society for change, the luxury and the conspicuous consump-

Carpenters at work.
Lorenzo Magalotti, Relazione di Svezia 1674.
Manuscript in the Uppsala University Library.
Photo: Uppsala University Library.

tion seem to have been the right medicine. Although there are many aspects that deserve more exhaustive research, it may be confirmed that the result was a long period of economic prosperity for many large and small merchants and for skilled craftsmen of all kinds, and also of high demand for certain agricultural products of the peasantry. The necessary resources were largely found within the country: hardly anybody managed to build

"with German money" and the significance of war booty has been wildly exaggerated. And even if there was an outflow of capital from Sweden for the purchase of foreign luxury goods and for the peregrinations of the young nobility, the majority must have benefitted the mother country. From this it follows that the consumption of luxuries must have resulted in a tremendous redistribution of wealth, which together with the growth

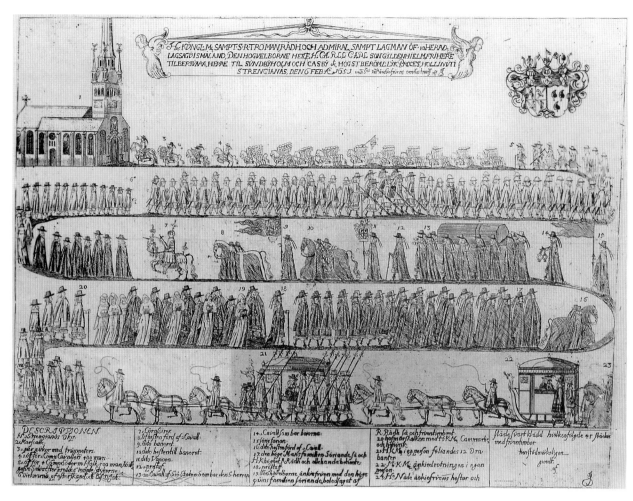

Funeral procession of Karl Karlsson Gyllenhielm to Strängnäs
Cathedral, 6 Februari 1651. Engraving by Johan Sass. Nordic
Museum.
Photo: Nordic Museum.

of the cash economy and the emergence of new social strata unattached to agriculture, served to expand the domestic market.

An Age of Change

During the years 1715–1720, the final years of absolutism and the Age of Greatness, the French traveller Aubry de la Motraye visited Sweden. Taking an interest in manners and customs, in topography and in monuments and other sights worthy of note, La Motraye had traversed Europe and also been in Africa and Asia. At Bender, in Turkey, he had met Karl XII. He took a good look at Sweden, and some of his impressions are worth recalling as illustrations of the changes that had taken place.

The Stockholm of the second decade of the eighteenth century was described by La Motraye as one of northern Europe's most beautiful cities, with broad, straight streets, fine public buildings, stately residences and large stone houses; it was a very different picture from that drawn by Ogier eighty years earlier, when the city still retained its medieval character. The Palace of the Nobility had now been in place for some considerable time, adorned with sculpture and legend, even if its interior was still unfinished. Work on the new royal palace had been interrupted by the war, but Tessin's residence was complete – "an architectural gem" in the opinion of La Motraye – and Carl Gustav Wrangel's palace had become the home of the royal family. And in the centre of Stockholm lay Kungsträdgården, a park of delightful flower beds, fountains and a superb orangery. So Sweden now had the capital city and the representative setting for the conducting of the state's affairs that the government had called for when Sweden first emerged as a great power. In the meantime, the city's population had grown explosively – from 10,000 in the 1620s to over 40,000, a figure already reached by the 1670s.

Turning to country houses, La Motraye was amazed that Sweden could have "so many castles and gardens of such beauty and splendour", bearing in mind the rugged landscape and the harsh winters. Not unexpectedly, he was most impressed of all with Drottningholm – by the palace's architecture, which was the work of Tessin the Elder; by the gardens, which had been laid by Tessin the Younger; and by Ehrenstrahl's paintings. In Tessin the Younger, it should be added, Sweden had an architect to whom foreign patrons, too, entrusted important commissions. The manor houses in other parts of the country were also praised by the Frenchman, notwithstanding the fact that they were generally of timber, which was regarded as a Swedish peculiarity. And even on the ironmasters' estates he found hothouses. It was, in other words, a striking architectural modernization that had belatedly taken place in Sweden.

At Uppsala La Motraye viewed the anatomical theatre, the collection of curiosities and mathematical instruments and the magnificent curio cabinet with which Gustav II Adolf had been presented by the city of Augsburg, and of course the Silver Bible. He particularly admired the fair-sized university library and its librarian, Eric Benzelius the Younger. It may be worthy of mention – although La Motraye was unaware of it – that a few years earlier Benzelius, who was a humanist with a strong interest in science and mathematics, had founded Sweden's first learned society at the instigation of the celebrated mathematician, inventor and industrial pioneer Christoffer Polhammar, later ennobled as Polhem. This was the first in a series of efforts to establish an academy that preceded the foundation of the Royal Swedish Academy of Sciences in 1739.

In the economic sphere La Motraye's interest was attracted primarily by the mines and the ironworks, whose prosperity in the seventeenth century was to a considerable degree the work of immigrants. Having started purely as a munitions industry, the ironworks had not been short of customers and Swedish ironmaking had attracted the interest of other countries. But the iron manufactories did not only produce arms: La Motraye also mentions factories engaged in civil production, particularly the one founded by Polhem at

Stjärnsund in 1699. Of the factory's many products he confines himself to the cups, plates, spoons etc. of tin-plate; these were made with the aid of a hydraulic machine that was operated by four people and did the work of thirty. The machine, which was the invention of Polhem, made a strong impression on the Frenchman, whose reflections we will now leave.

A Swedish production of artefacts of this type would have been inconceivable in the early years of the great-power period, given the country's undeveloped social and economic structure. But with the advent of the international aristocratic culture and the new luxury consumption a process of development began that entailed not only a dramatic increase in the demand for luxury goods in the strict sense but also an expansion of the domestic market generally. This had to happen before a domestic production of goods could come about. Another prerequisite was the transfer of wealth – a result of the luxury consumption – to bourgeois and newly ennobled circles with a more "modern" approach to the utilization of resources than that generally displayed by the nobility. The powerful merchant Roquette (Häger-stierna), for example, who was more aware than most of the size of demand, invested in brass and leather manufacture and in 1669 the descendants of Spiring (Silfvercrona), whom we recall from the New Sweden venture, were granted the monopoly right to manufacture linen in the province of Halland. A change in the attitude of the nobility to investment of this kind would not in fact be long in coming, as may be seen from the participation of various aristocrats in the Kungsholm Glassworks during the last decades of the seventeenth century and the involvement of the Estate of the nobility in a clothing factory early in the eighteenth.

The results of the extensive establishment of manufacturing industry which, encouraged and supported by the government, took place in the second half of the seventeenth century were not, of course, particularly impressive by comparison with what happened in the more developed countries of Western Europe, where this type of production had a long history. Many of the

Goblet bearing monogram of Karl XI, made at the Kungsholm Glassworks.
Photo: The National Swedish Art Museums.

projects had great difficulties to contend with, particularly the investment in the manufacture of silk, to which considerable resources were committed. But in relation to Swedish circumstances, and especially to the limited demand in the initial phase, the results were nonetheless remarkable.

These events formed the background to the founding in 1731 of the Swedish East India Company (initially almost an English business), which was successfully to trade Swedish ironware for tons of luxury goods such as tea, china and silk. It also formed the background to Anders Johan von Höpken's choice of subject for his presidential address in 1740 to the newly formed Swedish Academy of Sciences, which was entitled *Om yppighets nytta* ("On the benefits of luxury"). With this address Höpkens introduced to Sweden one of the most discussed problems of the age. In it he argued that in considering the effects of vanity and abundance the economies of private households and individuals had to be distinguished from society's and the public good. While the demand for luxury goods could certainly bring personal ruin, there was no doubt that it constituted an important stimulus to handicrafts, industry and science (including agricultural economics and navigation), and consequently to society as a whole. Höpken concluded by praising the way of life of the rich and self-indulgent Croesus, who squandered his inherited fortune on building and decorating houses, as well as on gorgeous clothing, coaches, feasts and gifts – an example that he probably drew from Voltaire. Even if the Swedish nobleman was not directly intended, this is not an inaccurate description of what many had tried to do. And to judge from the evidence this played an important role in the "civilizing" of Sweden.

References

This article is based on current research, of which I have rendered an account in two previous essays. See: Revera, M., "1600-talsbönderna och deras herrar", in *Rättshistoriska studier* (Series II) Volume IX, (Stockholm, 1984); also "En barock historia", in *Tre Karlar* (Stockholm, 1984). For other literature the reader is referred to these essays and to the preceding essays in this volume.

See also:

Ahnlund, N., "Nya Sverige i den historiska litteraturen", in *Historisk Tidskrift* (Stockholm, 1938).

Gardiner, S., *Evolution of the House* (London, 1975).

Hildebrand, B., *Kungl. Svenska Vetenskapsakademien* (Stockholm, 1939).

von Höpken, A.J., *Skrifter*, published by Carl Silfverstolpe, Volume I (Stockholm, 1890).

Jacobsson, N., *Bland Svenskamerikaner och Gustavianer* (Linköping, 1953).

Johnson, A., *The Swedish Settlements on the Delaware, 1638–1664*, Vols I–II (1911) (New York, 1970).

Lindahl, G., *Universitetsmiljö* (Uppsala, 1957).

Seigneur A. de la Motrayes resor 1711–1725, selected and translated by Hugo Hultenberg (Stockholm, 1918).

Sandström, Å., "Minuit, Peter", in *Svenskt Biografiskt Lexikon* XXV, p. 524 f (Stockholm, 1986).

Wieselgren, O., *Yppighets nytta* (Uppsala, 1912).